Make Money With Digital Marketing

A Supercharged Social Media Marketing Guide Of 2020. The Simple Way To Understand Money Management And How To Use The Latest Ideas Of Passive Income

By: Oliver J. Rich

Introduction 16

Chapter 1: Introduction to Digital Marketing............................ 19

Traditional Versus Digital Marketing 19

Importance of Digital Marketing 20

    Reaches a Wider Audience 20

    Allows Personalized Marketing 20

    Increases Mobile Transactions 21

    Increases Brand Awareness for Small Companies 21

    Easy to Use and Budget 22

Basics of Digital Marketing 22

    Business Idea and Plan 23

    A Business Name 24

    Business Theme Colors 24

    A Logo and Slogan 25

    The Service Analyzed 25

    Or, the Product Ready 26

    Set a Team of Professional Workers 27

    Business Registration and Licenses 27

    Competitor Analysis 28

    Web Copy and Content for Marketing 28

    Domain and Hosting 28

    A Website Platform and a Website 29

    Social Media Pages 29

    An Email Subscription SaaS 29

    Payment Methods Sorted 30

    At least 3 Email Addresses 30

Tips for Running a Successful Business Online 31
    Equip Your Website 31
    Customer Relationship 32
    Frequently Market Your Brand 34
    Keep Improving Your Brand 35
The Role of a Digital Marketer 36
    Create and Upload Product Images on the Company's Website 36
    Conduct Email Marketing Campaigns 36
    Conducts Analysis and Provide an Accurate Report on Return on Investment 37
    Research New Online Media Opportunities That May Favor the Business 37
    Designing Website Banners and Web Visuals 37
    Communicate with Clients and Affiliate Networks 38
    Monitor the Performance of Client Websites Through Web Analytics Software 38
    Initiate Lead Generation and Manage the Contact Database 38
    Contribute to Brand Awareness Campaigns and Social Media Engagement 38
    Negotiate with Media Suppliers to Achieve Favorable Prices for Your Clients. 39
Skills Required for a Digital Marketer 39
    Pay-Per-Click (PPC) Knowledge 39
    Content Creation and Marketing 39
    Social Media Specialist 40
    Business Strategy and Planning 41
    Analytical Skills 41
    Search Engine Optimization 41

    Communication and Leadership Skills 42

  Career Profiles in Digital Marketing 42

    Content Marketing Manager... 42

    Digital Analyst... 43

    Search Engine Optimizer 44

    Social Media Expert 44

    Media Planner 45

    Graphic Designer 45

    Copywriter 46

    Website Developer.. 46

    Digital Marketing Manager.. 47

    Affiliate Marketer 47

Chapter 2: Crafting Your Marketing Strategy 49

    Set Your Mission and Your Goals. 51

    Establish Your KPIs.. 52

    Know Your Audience 52

    Asses Your Current Position 53

    Figure out the Best Content Channels 53

    Decide on Content Types. 54

    Identify and Allocate Resources... 54

    Create a Content Calendar 54

    Create Content.. 55

    Distribute and Market 55

    Measure Results 55

  How to Conduct Competitive Analysis 56

    Identify Your Top Ten Competitors 56

    Analyze and Compare Competitor Content 57

- Analyze Their SEO Structure 58
- Look at Their Social Media Integration 58
- Identify Areas of Improvement 59

How to Target and Acquire Customers Online 60
- Use Google In-Market Audiences 60
- Facebook Custom Audience 60
- Understand E-Commerce Audience 61
- Customer Surveys and Feedback 61
- Stalk Your Competitor 62
- Customer Segmentation 62
- Post Relevant Blog Posts 63
- Create Engaging Newsletters to Generate Leads 63
- Use the Right Influencers 64
- Re-Evaluate Your Marketing Efforts 64
- Add Chatbots to Your Site 64
- Start Tracking 65
- Using LinkedIn for Keyword Research 65

The Best Platforms for Your Online Business 66
- Facebook 67
- YouTube 68
- Instagram 69
- Twitter 69
- Pinterest 70
- LinkedIn 70
- Snapchat 72
- Reddit 72

Competitor Challenge 73

Chapter 3: Introduction to Social Media Marketing 75

Instagram Marketing Tools 75

Buffer 75

Sprout Social 76

Iconosquare 76

Repost for Instagram 77

Sendible 77

Community.it 78

TweetDeck 79

Awario 79

Click to Tweet 80

Facebook Marketing Tools 80

The Facebook Ads Manager 81

Qwaya 81

AdEspresso 82

Hootsuite Ads 83

AdStage 83

Social Media Trends to Apply 83

Chatbots and Messenger Integration 83

Social Media TV 84

Live Streaming Events 85

Ephemeral Content 85

Social Media Listening 86

Contextual Ads 86

Augmented Reality 86

Reasons Why Social Media Marketing Works 87

Is Ideal for Start-Up Companies 87

- *Allows the Business Owner to Reach a Specific Audience* 87
- *Helps to Create a Community* 88
- *Helps Appeal Better to Potential Clients* 88
- *Improves Your Search Engine Optimization and Website Traffic* 89
- *Helps the Business Get New Leads through Recommendations* 89
- *Connects Business Owners and Potential Clients Globally* 90
- *Helps to Position Your Business Authoritatively* 90
- *Helps Business Owners Increase Their Influence* 90
- Social Media Challenge 91

Chapter 4: Business on the Internet 92

- How to Sell Services Online 92
  - *Consider Your Service and Market* 92
  - *Build out Your Website* 93
  - *Create the Necessary Pages* 93
  - *Generate Traffic and Clients* 95
  - *Do the Work* 95
- E-Branding and Selling Products Online 96
  - *Quality and Sophistication* 96
  - *Engage with Them* 97
  - *Use Influencer Marketing* 97
  - *Efficient Customer Service* 97
- Selling Products Online 98
  - *Easy Purchase and Great Customer Service* 98
  - *Secure Your Site* 99
  - *Create a Great Delivery System* 99
  - *Optimize Your Product Page* 100
  - *Mobile-Friendly Website* 100

Chapter 5: Forms of Digital Marketing 101

- Track Your Progress 101
- Enhance Promotions 102
- Provide Social Proof 102
- Performance-based payments 103
- Scale Your Online Business. 103
- Website Sustainability 104
- Strong ROI 104
- Increase Sales. 105

Dropship Marketing 105
- Master the Art of Marketing 105

Introduction to Email Marketing 110
How Email Marketing Works 111
How often should you send emails? 112
- Do Not Subscribe a Client Without Their Consent 113
- Every Email Sent out Must Contain the "Unsubscribe" Button 113

Creating the Pop-Up Message 114
Sending Newsletters 116
Types of Email List Software 117
Online PR 118
- Differences between Online and Traditional PR 119
- What Does Digital PR Involve? 121
- The Goal of Digital PR 121
- How Digital PR Can Benefit Your Brand 122
- Repurpose Your Content 122
- The Difference Between Online PR and Marketing 123
- Get Started with a Digital PR Campaign 123

Inbound Marketing 123

    Difference Between Inbound Marketing and Outbound Marketing 124

How to Get Started with Inbound Marketing.. 127

Pay-Per-Click (PPC) Marketing.. 128

    Benefits of PPC... 129

    Main PPC Platforms 130

    Remarketing 131

    Traffic.. 131

    PPC with Google 132

Video Marketing 132

    Why You Should Use Video When Marketing Your Brand............... 133

    Types of Videos 134

    Creating a Video Marketing Strategy.. 135

    Types of Video Distribution Channels 137

Mobile App Marketing.. 137

    Showcase Products 138

    Push Notifications 138

    New Audience and Customer Prefer Using Mobile Phones 139

    Cultivate Customer Loyalty... 139

How to Market Your Mobile App 139

    Make Your App Visible in App Stores... 140

    Measure Your App KPI 141

    Market Early 141

    Get Reviews 141

    Social Media and Influencers 142

Chapter 6: Content Creation and Marketing 143

What is Branded Content? 143

    Differences Between Branded Content and Other Marketing Strategies 144

    Advantages of Branded Content 145

    Developing an Emotional Attachment Takes You to the Next Advantage. 145

    Brands That Have Successfully Used Branded Content 146

  Content Writing for Brand Building 147

    What is Copywriting? 148

    What is SEO? 149

    How Does SEO Come in Content Writing? 149

Chapter 7: Enabling Your Sales Team 150

    Provide Training 150

    Keep Them in the Loop 151

    Reference a Script 151

    Create a Sales Playbook for Them 152

  Understanding Customer Intent 152

Chapter 8: Developing Your Brand Experience 154

  Create Fluid Content 154

  Build a Fluid and Dynamic Media 155

  Incorporate Swag 156

  Hold Events to Spearhead Your Marketing Efforts 156

  Why Gamification Works Well In Enhancing Brand Experience 157

  Hold a Social Media Consumer Contest 158

  Engagement 158

Chapter 9: Tracking Your Marketing Efforts with Google Analytics 160

  Importance of using Google analytics 160

    Audience Analysis 160

Measure the Effectiveness of Content 161

Track Social Media Presence 161

Track on Site User Behavior 161

How to Set Up and Use Google Analytics 162

Set Up Conversion Goals 162

How Google Analytics Works 163

Chapter 10: Growing Your Brand 164

Find out What Consumers Are Craving 164

   Keeping Up with Technology 164

Go Back to Your Strategic Plan 165

Incorporate More Things as You Go 165

Brand Growth Beginner Challenge 166

Chapter 11: Advantages of Social Media Marketing for Business 167

Social Media Marketing Guide for Beginners 172

   Facebook 173

   Blogs 174

   Twitter 176

   Linkedin 177

   YouTube 178

   Google+ 179

Social Media Statistics 180

Search Engine Optimization (SEO) details 181

The Impact of Social Media Marketing on Tourism 182

Problem Statement 185

Purpose of the study 187

   Methodology 188

   Findings 188

How to Boost Your Business With Standardization of Responses 189

Towards better customer experience 197

Boost Your Business Profits Even in Tough Times 197

Quick and Easy Ways to Boost Your Business Profits........................... 203

Ways To Boost Your Business With Teleseminars................................. 208

Chapter 12: Facebook Marketing Tips for Business 213

Advertising tips : 215

    1. The Photo Strip is at the top of your tab. 215

    2. Links to the left side of your page. 215

    3. Make the most of Facebook iFrames by adding exciting content. 216

    4. Updates functionality provides the opportunity for free advertising on valuable Facebook real estate. 216

    5. Improve awareness and interaction with Facebook News Feeds. 217

Facebook Marketing Ideas and Tools 218

Chapter 13: Instagram Marketing Tips for Your Business 227

Use quality media 228

Connect with our supporters 228

Use Hashtags 229

Use branded hashtag 229

Have a friendly attitude to everyone 229

Be active 230

Consistency 230

Link your Instagram and Facebook accounts 230

How to Use Instagram With Your Direct Sales Business 231

Start with your schooling. 235

Give a variety of leads. 235

Repetition. 235

Chapter 14: Pinterest Marketing 239

Pinterest Marketing Tricks 247

Chapter 15: Twitter Marketing **254**

Seven Free Twitter Marketing Strategies 269

Final Exercise 275

Conclusion **275**

© **Copyright 2019 - All rights reserved.**

This eBook is provided with the sole purpose of providing relevant information on a specific topic for which every reasonable effort has been made to ensure that it is both accurate and reasonable. Nevertheless, by purchasing this eBook you consent to the fact that the author, as well as the publisher, are in no way experts on the topics contained herein, regardless of any claims as such that may be made within. As such, any suggestions or recommendations that are made within are done so purely for entertainment value. It is recommended that you always consult a professional prior to undertaking any of the advice or techniques discussed within.

This is a legally binding declaration that is considered both valid and fair by both the Committee of Publishers Association and the American Bar Association and should be considered as legally binding within the United States.

The reproduction, transmission, and duplication of any of the content found herein, including any specific or extended information would be done as an illegal act regardless of the end form the information ultimately takes. This includes copied versions of the work both physical, digital, and audio unless the express consent of the Publisher is provided beforehand. Any additional rights reserved.

Furthermore, the information that can be found within the pages described forthwith shall be considered both accurate and truthful when it comes to the recounting of facts. As such, any use, correct or incorrect, of the provided information will render the Publisher free of responsibility as to the actions taken outside of their direct purview. Regardless, there are zero scenarios where the original author or the Publisher can be deemed liable in any fashion for any damages or hardships that may result from any of the information discussed herein.

Additionally, the information in the following pages is intended only for informational purposes and should thus be thought of as universal. As befitting its nature, it is presented without assurance regarding its prolonged validity or interim quality. Trademarks that are mentioned are done without written consent and can in no way be considered an endorsement from the trademark holder.

Introduction

Congratulations on purchasing "Make Money With Digital Marketing", and thank you for dedicating your time and energy into this.

The following chapters will discuss digital marketing as the ultimate tool for succeeding online as a business. The internet reportedly has over 4 billion current users worldwide. But unlike Facebook's CEO, Mark Zuckerberg, hundreds of thousands of online companies are tanking and barely making three figures in sales (let alone profits) annually. The difference can be narrowed down to two simple things; brand quality and marketing strategies.

There is a high chance that your product has better quality than that of a famous company. Sadly, this does not mean that people will leave such companies to buy from you. On the other hand, fantastic marketing strategies do not achieve much if the quality of the products or services provided is low. In this handbook, you learn how to get both those factors right to improve your chances of success.

Thus far, you can tell that digital marketing is a whole basket of tasks that requires a team of professionals to run. However, as a start-up, you can either outsource some of the digital marketing services or invest in a bit more time learning and doing it by yourself. That is what this handbook is offering you — a chance to know what this prolific skill entails and how to brand your business to success.

There are plenty of books on this subject on the market; thanks again for choosing this one! Every effort was made to ensure it is full of as much useful information as possible; please enjoy!

Chapter 1: Introduction to Digital Marketing

Digital marketing is all about reaching out to potential customers, converting them, and retaining them using the internet and its tools. Whether your business offers products or services, you can still use various technologies to promote and make popular your brand.

Traditional Versus Digital Marketing

Both of these methods rely on similar marketing concepts – finding and keeping customers. The main difference between traditional and digital marketing is the tools used. With traditional marketing, corporates use radio, television ads, newspapers and magazines, business cards and brochures, billboards, and the like. With digital marketing, online platforms like social media pay per click advertising, emails, websites, search engines and visual representations like videos and graphics are used. As much as digital marketing has become more popular over time, corporates are still using traditional methods to advertise their brand. Traditional marketing is not going away in 2020 or even 5 years to come.

Importance of Digital Marketing

What are the main reasons why you should incorporate digital marketing into your business plan?

Reaches a Wider Audience

With the use of digital platforms, business owners not only communicate to their targeted audience but also reach a wider audience. Traditional methods, on the other hand, though an essential tool in reaching a specific audience does not attract new clients. For instance, if you are using a business magazine to advertise your business, then you are likely to communicate with the magazine readers only.

Allows Personalized Marketing

This is mostly made possible by using an email listing; studies have revealed about 70% of consumers prefer communication with service and product providers through emails. Personalized digital marketing also increases repeat clients.

Furthermore, email listings are also an essential tool in providing new information to customers; this also keeps businesses ahead and invested in growth as customers can opt-out of the email subscription at any time.

Increases Mobile Transactions

There is a 35% increase in sales each year through mobile phones. Prospects can now view, share, and even buy at their convenience; someone could be in the park and simply recommend a product or shop on their phone.

Increases Brand Awareness for Small Companies

For years now, the huge companies have dominated in business, and this has led to the closure of several stores, this is due to many years of marketing and branding, making it hard for the upcoming business to enter the market.

Fortunately, digital marketing has brought hope for these enterprises. Through digital marketing, small companies can create their voice in the market; in turn, it increases trust and credibility. In addition, there are various angles when it comes to improving a brand through digital marketing; business owners can create open forums, where clients can ask questions or present issues. By responding to the clients, business owners show their commitment to the clients as well as build their brand.

Additionally, digital marketing showcases reviews, which play a big part in influencing customers decisions, studies have revealed that about 70% of potential clients on digital platforms get recommendations from family and friends who have transacted with a particular business.

Easy to Use and Budget

Some of the popular digital marketing platforms include; Facebook, Instagram, Email listing, Twitter, and Pinterest, to mention a few. By using a platform such as Facebook, you get to manage and monitor money spent on marketing, and this is made possible by the low advertisements cost; a Facebook ad may cost as low as $11, amounting to less than $80 in a week. The advertisements are not altered, and one gets to decide when to post the ad. If for example, the statistics show your business is not doing well, then you can take a break as you change your marketing plans.

Basics of Digital Marketing

Digital marketing involves a combination of online platforms, tools, written and visual content, a brand, and the public. This means you need all the above to successfully run an online business. There are two types of businesses, those that run purely online and those that also run on brick and motor. Both types of businesses use the same rules when it comes to branding and marketing their products or services.

To launch a business online, you need a few basics for your online business foundation. Some of these items you may already have if your business runs on brick or motor. Either way, it is important to take note.

Business Idea and Plan

Before getting started, you need a viable business idea. This can be derived from acquired knowledge, skills, hobbies, or a passion. Analyze your business idea according to the current market. Is the demand for that product or service high? Is supply for the same high as well? If it is a new concept in the market, what problems does it solve and how well does it solve them? Never rush the idea phase. This is where many loopholes arise. Keep in mind that the idea is for the customers and not for you; therefore, it has to satisfy your future audience filled to the brim. If there are other similar brands in the market, find your unique identifier. Something has to make you stand out before the crowd; otherwise, your idea will not achieve much. Do not stress looking for perfection; there is always room for improvement and updates as you go.

Then comes the business plan. This is where you put your ideas into practice but on paper. Analyze everything from the problem being addressed, the solution you will provide and step by step representation of how it will work, and its strengths and weaknesses, and the target audience as well. Have a budget for all business requirements and a strategic plan for how you will run and grow your business. The plans you make must be realistic, but not comfortable. Challenge yourself. Do not rush the idea and planning phase. Even if it takes a year or more, be patient and as accurate as possible. This will help your business flourish faster once it starts off.

A Business Name

From the idea, you can come up with a good business name that fits. Your business name should be easy to pronounce and relatable, making it easily memorable. You can always outsource a copywriter to work on a few business name options for you. Copywriters are good at coming up with text that sells to your specific audience.

Business Theme Colors

These first few aspects are probably done for businesses that run on the ground. However, it is never too late to rebrand. Every business has their theme colors. It can be one color, two or a bunch of colors just like Google or Instagram's. The theme color will be used as identification on all your branding materials, including your logo and website. Pick colors that relate to your service. If you pick more than one color, ensure they blend in perfectly. A graphics designer can assist with color selection and coordination.

A Logo and Slogan

The next step is to get a logo designed. It is always advisable to outsource for a professional graphics designer. If you do not know one, you can filter freelancers from sites like Upwork, Fiverr, 99 Designs, or freelancer.com for as low as $5 to as high as $90, and get a good logo in a day or two.

As for the slogan, get a copywriter to create one that will sell your brand. All aspects of your business contribute to selling your brand, including tiny details like the name, logo, and slogan. Therefore, invest in them and they will go a long way. Get a second to tenth opinion if possible until you are satisfied with the logo and slogan.

The Service Analyzed

If you are working on a service, analyze how it will work. You have probably analyzed this in the business plan phase. However, in this step, you go deeper into details, explaining things like the sales process, and how you would like the website to achieve this. This phase is more about the website functioning. Your website will be your digital office; therefore, it has to achieve everything an actual office can achieve. This includes aspects like customer service, where online, you include a live chat.

Plan on until the last step of payment. While this might seem like a hustle, it helps you avoid confusion on the way, helps you appear organized and professional, and definitely makes the web design process that much easier since you now know the features you require on the website.

Or, the Product Ready

In case your business deals with products and not services, do the same analysis. From when the customer spots the product to how they purchase it and receive it at their doorstep. Ensure to analyze payment options, terms, and policies of payment as well. If a product is destroyed during shipping, if it is something that can go stale when transporting, if the customer receives the product but it does not work, how will you sort all those situations? What precautions will you take to ensure you avoid such situations? This step helps you cover all the loopholes that may cost your business.

Set a Team of Professional Workers

Now that you have analyzed the sales process, you are able to identify all the personnel required for your business. For example, at the consultation stage, you need a professional wedding consultant. If that is not you, then fill that position. When the client makes the payment, you need someone to record that in your accounting software. Hire an accountant or a secretary for that. Look into every stage and ensure you have personnel for each step. Remember your customer service representative must be able to stay online throughout your working hours. This will make communication efficient.

Business Registration and Licenses

Unlike brick and motor businesses, online businesses do not require as many licenses to run. However, it is important to register your business, make it legal, and under the IRS as well to ensure you pay taxes. If your profession requires a license to practice, ensure you have one before you begin. Such documents bring a business to the forefront in terms of legitimacy.

Competitor Analysis

Before getting into the nitty-gritty of your business setup, look at what your competitors are up to. This will help you create the right path for your business. Who is your competitor? As a startup, you can look at any running business. However, it is better to aim at the sky by analyzing businesses that are ruling the industry. This way, you will launch your online business on a high note.

Web Copy and Content for Marketing

Your website content is the content that is found on the home page, about page, services page, and contacts page. Write this content beforehand. Many assume the basic website content, but it is important to note that when done right, website content can rank your website on Google. Being a copy (the text that sells your brand), it is advisable to hire a professional copywriter to work on it.

Domain and Hosting

Buy a domain and hosting to get space and a name for your website. There are many affordable service providers of domain and hosting. Others charge on a monthly basis and others annually. Get a plan that works best for you.

A Website Platform and a Website

Whether you are using Shopify, WordPress, Divi, Wix and such platforms, know which one is easier to use with a great user interface and features that will serve your business well. Pick a theme that will represent your business with elegance and attract prospects. Customize the theme to resemble your ideal corporate theme.

Social Media Pages

Open social media pages that you will use to update and communicate with your prospects. Your social media pages must contain bio information that coincides with your website copy. Your logo must occupy the profile picture section, and an attractive design to feature in the cover image section. Remember to use your official business name as your social media page name.

An Email Subscription SaaS

Sign up to one of the readily available email newsletter platforms. If you have a few emails for friends and family or previous clients, you can request their consent to add them as your first subscribers.

Payment Methods Sorted

If you choose to manage your payments online, then you had better sort your payment methods before launching your business. Being unable to make payments makes customers really frustrated and disappointed with your services.

At least 3 Email Addresses

From the hosting platform, set up at least 3 email addresses. One for customer service, and the other two depending on your business model. Have a separate social media email so that social updates and notifications can be sent separately from your daily business.

Tips for Running a Successful Business Online

The Internet does have over 4 billion users currently, but this has not been a guarantee that all online businesses will meet their success. Just like bricks and mortars, an effort has to be made, strategies used and goals targeted. Just because you may work remotely, does not make it any easier. Business rules and marketing efforts - not forgetting customer relationship management - are all required in your business journey.

Now, assuming that you have perfected your product or service to ensure you have nothing but quality, here are 10 tips to ensure your online business is successful.

Equip Your Website

This is your online office and should have all the business equipment installed. For an online business, that would mean having:

- Social media icons for easy access

- A contacts page with the company's physical address (if any), email contact form, telephone number, and email address
- A live chat for faster customer service
- An easy to use website with clear font, images, and an attractive interface
- Detailed information on each offered service
- An e-commerce page for product brands
- A pop-up box for collecting emails
- An about page that tells a client more about the company
- Price lists or pricing tables that break down offered packages and gives amount for each package

Let the website have all the required information to be able to sell your products and services for you. A vague website will increase click-through rate, decreasing your chances of conversion.

Customer Relationship

Whether you are achieving this through social media or your website, be sure to pamper your customers and prospects as much as possible. Obviously, they will either build or break your business, making you have fewer options. The greatest challenge many online businesses face today is the social media backlash. You work on a campaign or product, put all your time and effort, then it backfires to your face. The ability for people to discuss and influence each other on certain matters, freely on social media, has become a breaking point for businesses. This means that before you launch a product or service, analyze it thoroughly. Send out a demo to a few prospects - if possible - and get their opinion.

Say a campaign backfires on you, it is important to address the issue in an honest and professional way. However, keep it sensible. Just because you do not see a problem with your product, does not mean there is none. This applies to customers unsatisfied with your service. Make an effort to apologize, explain yourself so that the customer can understand where you were coming from, and offer them an incentive to show them that they matter to you.

Dealing with customers is a great challenge, but just like face-to-face services, you need to be keen and highly sensitive to their complaints. Remember, the customer is always right.

Frequently Market Your Brand

If you are looking to escape marketing, you have a long way to go. Not to say that you cannot succeed without promotions, but to say that you have slim chances and you are rolling the dice on them. Social media is the main method of marketing that an online business should apply. It is not always pocket change projects, sometimes-daily posts and blogs attract new prospects and convert them to customers. Actually, most of the time, content is what sells your service and product. Therefore, blog about your industry, post images and videos of your product and get conversations going in online groups, forums, pages, and the like.

Use Google AdWords to advertise using search engine optimization. Run campaigns and competitions to get traffic to your site and popularize your product. A few good collaborations with reputable brands will not hurt a bit. Just ensure that the brands are not competitors.

For Example;

If your business sells coffee, you can run a collaborated campaign with a milk brand and show people the numerous ways to enjoy white coffee.

When marketing, invest in professional skills of copywriting and graphic design. Make your posts count and your message passed across in an informative but entertaining way.

Keep Improving Your Brand

Do not rebrand on a regular, but do so when need be. The internet is growing way too fast. The trick that worked today may end up being irrelevant tomorrow. This means you have to be on top of your game and the first to apply trending tools and methods online. Google and social media algorithms keep changing as well. It helps to keep in touch with updates that will save you from wasted marketing efforts that were not meant to work to begin with. Also, regularly analyze your competitors. When they pick up a new marketing style, learn about it and apply it in a unique way to avoid looking like a copy.

Improving your brand also means releasing product and service updates regularly. As no brand is perfect, it is essential to show your audience that you care for them, and go a mile to make their experience better. Advertise every update you release to maintain your customers and keep new ones coming. This is where email lists come in handy. Send emails with product updates and get your dormant clients shopping again.

Monitoring your business performance using tools like Google Analytics helps you know how far back you have fallen and what your strong points are. Check your analytics at least once each week so that you can spot a loophole fast and fix it before it affects your business. You can also review sales over time and see what campaigns are bringing in sales and what you are wasting your efforts on.

Running an online business is not an easy task that can be done with one hand. As your business grows, even during startup stages, you will need to outsource or hire a team of professionals to help run things smoothly and effectively.

The Role of a Digital Marketer

Create and Upload Product Images on the Company's Website

Only quality aesthetic images that represent the company's brand and goals should be uploaded on the website.

Conduct Email Marketing Campaigns

This is sending emails to prospective customers through a pre-prepared email list with the goal of marketing your products.

The goal is to make the customer take action, provide more leads, and increase sales.

Conducts Analysis and Provide an Accurate Report on Return on Investment

This involves creating reports on market performance, benchmarking your brand against market competitors, and giving recommendations on how to achieve the best in the market.

Research New Online Media Opportunities That May Favor the Business

This involves adopting the creation of new blogs in line with your marketing goals. Consider venturing to more social media platforms and online forums for maximum customer engagement.

Designing Website Banners and Web Visuals

You should be able to create effective web banners and visuals that drive traffic to the site while advertising the company's products and services.

Communicate with Clients and Affiliate Networks

This involves providing important information to potential and current customers through respective communication and liaising with affiliate partners and networks who share a common goal.

Monitor the Performance of Client Websites Through Web Analytics Software

This is used to collect present data on website users, through measuring web traffic as a tool for market research.

Initiate Lead Generation and Manage the Contact Database

This is maintaining a contact list for potential clients and partners while initiating consumer interests into products and services.

Contribute to Brand Awareness Campaigns and Social Media Engagement

This is increasing the viability of your products and services while engaging your customers on social media for maximum feedback.

Negotiate with Media Suppliers to Achieve Favorable Prices for Your Clients.

This is requesting for discounted rates for your clients by engaging the suppliers on their behalf.

Skills Required for a Digital Marketer

Pay-Per-Click (PPC) Knowledge

The responsibility of a pay per click specialist is to drive traffic to your site. You should be well versed in advertising and be able to manage all pay per click campaigns. You must be able to apply keywords basics and Search engine optimization for maximum engagement. For this to be successful, you need to understand current market trends and be able to work under pressure.

Content Creation and Marketing

This is a key aspect of digital marketing, and therefore, expertise in writing content for blog posts and social media is a must-have. To become a content marketing manager, you need to have knowledge of multimedia marketing strategies' content creators should be able to offer high-quality content in line with the brand's strategic plan and the company's marketing goals. Being able to use different media types for engagement, e.g., text, video, audio, and images, is an added advantage.

Social Media Specialist

A social media specialist should be able to carry out audience research and come up with a social media strategy. This will help in achieving maximum customer engagement while understanding how each social media works. You should be able to set up and optimize company social media pages to increase website traffic and visibility.

Business Strategy and Planning

For you to take up a leadership role in digital marketing, it is necessary to have a background in business. Long term planning allows for strategies and resource allocation to be aligned with company goals.

Analytical Skills

As much as it is necessary to access and research data, it is equally important to analyze and report on it. Being able to use technology in data analysis is an advantage since it is not necessarily integrated into the marketing programs in the university. As much as you may have a business and creative background, being analytic pays more since it comes from advanced education. Analytics are used to access sales and generate digital campaign results.

Search Engine Optimization

For you to be an SEO expert, you may need a background in web development. Your job will involve the use of data and understanding how numbers relate to business goals and marketing strategy. Having a basic understanding of how to translate and report data is critical in being able to report to your team.

Communication and Leadership Skills

Being able to communicate and create relationships with people is important in digital marketing. You should be able to lead and follow through all tasks as much as most of your roles are technical if you are looking at managerial roles; this skill is quite relevant to enhance teamwork.

Career Profiles in Digital Marketing

If you are a business owner or service provider, then one marketing strategy to use is the digital marketing, this advertisement technique not only addresses a large audience but is also an ideal option for small and medium businesses.

To better understand what you may be lacking in your digital marketing team or career paths in digital marketing. Below is a list of top digital marketing career profiles.

Content Marketing Manager

When it comes to digital marketing, content is on top of the list, and research has shown authentic and informative content leads to an increase in sales. Thus making content marketing manager a lucrative job.

A content marketing manager is tasked with managing websites and blogs, video ads, and email communications. The required skill set for content marketing manager include copywriting abilities, editing, have an understanding of SEO, strong research skills, and have a proficiency in English.

Additionally, a content marketing manager works closely with graphic designers, photographers, and writers, thus essential to have excellent communication skills.

A content marketing manager makes around $14 to $40 in an hour.

Digital Analyst

The second career on the list is a digital analyst. A digital analyst is tasked with marketing campaigns. Before embarking on digital marketing, it is essential to understand what will work for your business. The digital analyst looks at what social media platforms will work best, SEO techniques to use for various projects, and later examines the performances of the marketing techniques to find out the efficiency or changes needed.

To become a digital analyst, one needs to have strong research skills and a great understanding of social media platforms.

A digital analyst earns between $12 to around $63 hourly, but most digital analysts receive an average of $42 hourly.

Search Engine Optimizer

Want your website to rank high? Then you might need a search engine optimizer. Search engine optimizers specialize in increasing website ratings by improving the appearance of the site and making use of keywords.

A search engine optimizer will help your site get organic traffic, but you need to part with about $12 to $27 an hour's work. Some of the skills to look out for when hiring a search engine optimizer include; a good command of English, a great understanding of search engine optimization techniques and algorithms.

Social Media Expert

Social media marketing platforms take up a large part when it comes to digital marketing. Thus necessary to have a social media expert, a social media expert as the name suggests deals with managing social media business pages to influence discussions, build a brand, and attract customers.

To become a social media expert; be knowledgeable on social media platforms, one also needs to be creative and have strong interpersonal skills.

Social media specialists earn an average of $14 an hourly rate, while the average yearly salary is $50, 400.

Media Planner

Media planners help to keep track of expenses and estimating how much sales certain digital marketing techniques will generate. To become a media planner, one needs to be proficient in accounting, possess excellent communication skills, and have an understanding of digital marketing platforms.

A media planner earns averagely $18 in an hour, with most media planner receiving an average of $49, 400 yearly.

Graphic Designer

For digital marketing, it is essential to brand your business, and one way to stand out as a brand is by using unique logos, advertisement layout pictures, and interfaces and this is made possible by graphic designers.

Some of the skill sets required to become a graphic designer include; background in multimedia, be creative and open-minded, as market needs change each day.

Graphic designers receive an estimated $44, 300 yearly, while part-time designers charge around $17 hourly rate.

Copywriter

Can your words capture someone's attention or influence a sale? Then copywriting may be the job for you. Copywriters offer email marketing reads, blogging and website content and social media marketing content

Copywriters need to have exceptional organizational and research skills, a great understanding of keywords and SEO, and be creative. Copywriters, receive an hourly fee of around $28, while experienced copywriters charge up to $49 hourly.

Website Developer

Another lucrative opportunity in digital marketing is working as a website developer. Many businesses now have online stores, thus an increasing need for websites. If you are not tech-savvy, then sourcing for a website developer is the way to go.

To be a website developer, one needs to know HTML and CSS, Photoshop, JavaScript, SEO, and have strong analytical skills. Website developers receive an average of $1000 to $3000 as a freelancer, while agencies charge $10,000 for a project. One can also charge hourly for approximately $30.

Digital Marketing Manager

A digital marketing manager has a broader job description as they are tasked with overseeing all matters concerning digital marketing. Requiring a digital marketing manager to work closely with social media managers, SEO experts, and digital analysts.

To become a successful digital marketing manager, it is essential to have strong leadership and interpersonal skills, a proper understanding of social media platforms, Google Analytics, and their algorithms.

A digital marketing manager receives approximately $73,100 in a year, while the salary can go as high as $104,000 in a year. However, new digital marketing managers should expect to earn around $50,000 a year.

Affiliate Marketer

Affiliate marketing is one of the moneymaking techniques used in e-commerce. Affiliate marketers are thus tasked with managing the relationship between companies and affiliate partners.

To become an affiliate marketer, some of the skills required include, negotiation and analytical skills and strong knowledge in database technology. Affiliate marketers earn an average of $42, 000 a year.

Note: Hourly, monthly, and yearly charges in all these careers vary and are mostly influenced by one's experience, the popularity of your brand, region, and the complexity of the work. Fortunately, digital marketing careers do not limit workers to 9 to 5 timelines. One can opt to offer their services as a freelancer on both part-time and full-time contracts.

Chapter 2: Crafting Your Marketing Strategy

Content strategy is the act of managing all the information that you put out there concerning your company. The content created, however, needs to be marketed so that it can reach a wider audience. Content marketing is a continuous process. Business people need to change with time and adopt current methods of marketing. Previous ways that you were using may still be working, but for you to attract newer and more customers, you will need to revise your strategy. Including technologies that are more recent in your plan will help you capture the newer generation of your customers. A budget for the marketing should always be accounted for, most successful companies' records using up to 40 percent of their budgets on content marketing.

Businesses create different types of content to use in advertising their brand. Some of the content produced is in the form of:

- *Articles.* Companies need to publish their news and stories. Companies can create materials that are available to the public and offer information they would like to reach the audience. From the articles, they can even advertise their products.

- *Podcasts.* There are multiple sites where you can record yourself and post your content. Audio content is more comfortable to consume since it does not require as much concentration as reading.

- *Blog posts.* Blogs have different types of useful information that can be very useful to the reader. The company can provide life hacks and empower its consumers while delivering helpful information relating to the product they are selling. Such information is likely to promote your products more.

- *Case studies are another form.* It is in text form for video footage. They show how a client was facing a problem, and once they changed and started using your product, their life has not been the same. Prospective customers are likely to start using the product after receiving this kind of content.

- *Newsletters.* Newsletters explain recent activities that have been happening in your company in a short document while delivering the maximum amount of content they can. Newsletters can also be used to show events coming up soon. Newsletters are also popular nowadays since they are in soft copy form.

- *Photos.* High quality and custom pictures to feature the brand are markets the product more as compared to stock photos. Photoshoots can be organized by the company to come up with this content. The images can be pictures, memes, or gifs, which are prevalent in most social media platforms.

- The above mentioned are just a few of the types of content that companies use. For the best outcome, you can combine two or three at once. With a little expertise to ensure, the message is delivered and all questions that the customer has are answered.

After the content is ready, it will need distributing. Content distributors have come up to ease this task for companies. Some of the conventional content distributors are press release companies, brand partnership companies, and social media marketing. For you to market your content effectively, you need a plan. Some of the steps you can follow to execute a perfect marketing plan are below.

Set Your Mission and Your Goals.

Coming up with a goal and a mission for your strategy is the first step to winning. It helps to keep you in focus. You know what to focus on and what to ignore in this journey. It should have your target audience, the type of content you will use, and how you will be of use to the community. While the goals and missions may seem to focus your customers mainly, you should also think about how you will benefit from them. Once you have mastered your goal, you are bound to stay on track.

Establish Your KPIs

KPI is an antonym for Key Performance Indicators. The KPIs you use should be realistic. Your goals should be measurable so that it can be easy to track your progress. For your content marketing strategies, KPIs are vital since they show your targets by setting up numerical quantities for them. Some of the KPIs can be in terms of revenue, sales, and traffic. A tracking on expenditure is also essential to avoid unnecessary losses while still catering to all the needed expenses.

Know Your Audience

Researching your target market is essential. It helps you to coin the right type of content that will reach them in the most natural way possible and influence them. Some forms of conducting the research are.

You are collecting their demographic data. The data you need is their age, gender, education, interests, and income. This information is available from Google analytics.

Get customer feedback. Feedback is available if you interact with clients. From the information, you will know how the customers feel and how you can improve the experiences they have with your products.

Create buyer personas. You create buyer personas and show the ideal customer. Best personas show the problems encountered by your customers. With this information, you can target your customers better since you know the content your market likes and how it can be of use to them.

Asses Your Current Position

Your content is already out there. On your blogs or social media platforms. You need to check whether this content is meeting its intended goals or it needs to be improved. To know how your content is performing. You can compare it to that if your competitors, check if it is useful and its success rate and find any gaps present.

Figure out the Best Content Channels

By now, you have already established what triggers your target market. Since you already know the content, they like you should concentrate on that type of content. Focusing on one thing is more likely to bring success than focusing on many things at once. You should, therefore, focus on the areas that bring most returns and focus on improving them.

Decide on Content Types.

The best content marketing strategy is having the information being produced in a central place, then distributing it to your other marketing platforms. Induce different types of content to go with your primary material. You can include pictures and videos, which are more likely to engage your audience interactions.

Identify and Allocate Resources.

Since you know the content, you want to produce, and you should now allocate all the resources needed for it to be a success. You should assign roles in creating and managing the content, allocate the finances and tools you will need and understand how the content should flow.

Create a Content Calendar

The content created should be published at the appropriate time. You should have a plan on when you what to post your content. Answering your customers' questions is essential in creating the next content that you are going to publish. You can use software tools to plan for publishing if the content is a lot. Some of the tools you can use are Google calendar, Asana or Co-Schedule.

Create Content

Since you have an idea of the type of content you want to create, it is easier to create. Come up with a title for your content and start creating. Check on the material that is already available and analyze how the new content will fit. Ensure the further information adds value to your clients.

Distribute and Market

For the content to reach the audience, it needs to be well marketed. Whenever you release new material. Alert all your customers subscribed to email notifications and inform all your influencers. Start selling the product so it can reach the most massive audience possible.

Measure Results

Check your KPIs to see how far you have come. Check to see your progress from the new strategies that you have incorporated.

Incorporating new strategies for your marketing is bound to improve your results. Consider feedback from your customers and use it to create unique content. Always improving your content will make you attend to your clients more. Never settling is good, and using any item that will enhance your sales should be used to your advantage.

How to Conduct Competitive Analysis

Competitive analysis shows how unique your services are what attracts your clients to you. It enables you to know your position in the market. For you to conduct your analysis, you need to find out who your competitors are and how you are in competition with them. You should know the products they sell and how that affects your market share. Research and find out if as much information as you can about your competitors, such as their types of strategies in advertising, their strengths and weaknesses, and the threat they cause for you in the market. For you to make a clear comparison, you need to place your products in comparison to those of your competitors and see which ones your clients would prefer. However, for you to conduct a comprehensive analysis of your company, follow the steps below.

Identify Your Top Ten Competitors

A simple way to find your competitors is by looking for companies that sell the same kind of goods and services that you sell. Google is a good place to find this kind of information.

By simply googling, the kind of products and services that you sell you will easily find the companies that also sell the same. Your marketing team is the first department that notices competition, consulting them will give you a clear idea about who is your competition. No matter your location or size of the company you have, you are bound to have competitors. Finding your competitors is the first step towards conducting the analysis.

Analyze and Compare Competitor Content

After finding out the companies you are in competition with, you need to find out the type of content they are producing. The companies can be producing a different kind of content but they must have their main and most preferred kind. Analyze the quality of content they produce. Analyze your own quality of content then compare the two. A comparison between the qualities gives you a chance to make improvements and knowing how to improve. Improvement can be through more creativity or allocating more resources towards a certain area. From the information, you can also find out where you have the upper hand as compared to your competitors and use the information to your advantage.

Analyze Their SEO Structure

SEO stands for search engine optimization. SEO is common with companies that use blogs. It helps to optimize searches so your blog is easily available. You need to find out the types of keywords that your competitors use. Keywords can be placed in the title or body. Finding out how your competitors structure their keywords is also important. Search for words that have low search volumes rather than those with high search volumes. Low search volumes words tend to be more specific compared to those with high search volumes since they show general searches. The keywords your competitors use will give your ideas on words you can use to optimize your own searches. Also paying money into advertisements is a sure way to be among the top when searches are conducted.

Look at Their Social Media Integration

Social media presence is an important marketing strategy in today's world. It provides a platform to interact with your clients. It also allows you to post your content and to promote your sales. From social media, you can find a lot of information like how frequent the post, the number of interactions visible and the number of followers they have. From the information gathered, you could compare your brand with that of your competitors to see how you are doing and the improvements you need to apply. You can also learn new tactics of handling social media that your competitors may be using. Incorporating influencers in your social media campaigns is a sure way to jump-start your presence in the social media world.

Identify Areas of Improvement

After all the above steps, you have gathered a ton of information. From this information, it is easier to notice areas that may need improvement from your end. You can add new tactics to the tactics you were using that will help you improve and give you a better position in the market.

Competition is important for growth. You can have direct or indirect competition. However, checking how your competition is performing in the market is not illegal and can give you important information that you can use to your advantage. The above points are just a few areas you can compare yourself to your competitors. However, applying the tips and ensuring an improvement is a sure way of improving your sales and obtaining a better position in the market.

How to Target and Acquire Customers Online

Use Google In-Market Audiences

This is targeting your audience who are researching your services through a Google analytical report. Using the findings, you are able to create different ad groups in relation to the services that resonate with them. This becomes effective since it is backed up by the collected data. Using keyword matches, past searches, and the users browsing behavior, you can be able to predict what people are interested in. This is a practical customer acquisition plan that widens your reach and increases your sales.

Facebook Custom Audience

Since Facebook is a personalized data platform, it has a wide selection of formats to target reach and engage potential clients. Based on the user's interests, Facebook allows businesses to target users by providing only relevant ads. This allows businesses to create content that brings value to the consumer. Once a Facebook user engages with an advert, you send them another ad to capture more attention from them. The back-end ad platform on Facebook allows the advertiser to reach the right audience and track performance using cost per clicks and click through rates. You can get an analysis of which category of the audience is interested in your products and what cost it will take to reach them.

Understand E-Commerce Audience

The most common concern for an online business is a lot of irrelevant traffic on their site. This means that though you are able to drive a lot of traffic on your site, the conversion rate is very low in most cases. Using a good content strategy and basic S.E.O skills can get you many site visits, but they are irrelevant if nobody is making a purchase. Defining your e-commerce target audience saves time that was previously used to reach a bigger, less interested audience. This helps you use lesser resources to generate the same income since you are aware of your target audience needs

Customer Surveys and Feedback

When you speak to your customers, you are able to adapt the best business strategies from their input. It has become necessary to keep a record of customer feedback after transacting with them. This could involve putting up a brief survey for new users in order to capture their interests and preferences. Customer feedback can be graphically presented to measure success and improve business strategies. When you engage your customers often, you can request for product reviews on public rating forums.

Stalk Your Competitor

One of the online business best practices is to keep track of your competitors and their business strategies. This helps to discover which type of marketing strategy works and which one does not. Keep a record of products and services they offer and use their audience data to know what market you should take care of. Researching on your competitor gives you new ideas for your business and reveals their weaknesses. You may be providing the same products, but the use of different strategies may yield different results. Take advantage of their strategies to market your own products as you are all targeting the same market.

Customer Segmentation

This involves using demographical information such as name, age, and location to categorize your e-commerce audience. Take note of your customer's profession and lifestyle and use this to make informed business decisions. Survey your current customers in line with your target clients and find out how you can better present your products. Understand your target market by making individual profiles for all users that visit your site, and use this to create a target group for clients with similar needs. This is important while designing the right promotional material for your clients

Post Relevant Blog Posts

Make it a habit to publish original and relevant blog posts to educate your customers on your products and services. Focus on informational content, in regards to why your products are important and what value they add to the customer. Your blog post should be tailored to an audience in mind and be very specific. Inspire people to share your point of view while giving them valuable wisdom to solve industry-related problems. Make your content consistent even if it means outsourcing for content writers.

Create Engaging Newsletters to Generate Leads

Lead generation is the most time-consuming online marketing aspects. That is because it involves consumer analysis and online surveys that take a lot of time and resources. This, however, can be made easier by creating personalized newsletters and promotional campaigns that can be sent out via email. Ensure that your newsletter stimulates and captures interest to build a continuous relationship with your target. Having a solid lead generation plan will ensure that you establish trust with your client and increase sales.

Use the Right Influencers

To attract a wide share of the market, you will need to engage the best players in the industry. Using an influencer to market your products means that you are able to earn the trust of their fans and friends as well as establish credibility. Engage well-established bloggers by sending them relevant and informational content for your products and services. An influencer helps to build and improve your content strategy by bringing in new ideas to your business. The advantage of influencer marketing is that audiences are already available; you only need to find a way to foster a win-win relationship.

Re-Evaluate Your Marketing Efforts

This involves reviewing your business plan and strategy to measure effectiveness. Check whether your products add value and whether your customers appreciate them. Discover what affects your customer's decision to purchase your products and whether they are sustainable. This will help you improve your business strategy in line with your target audience.

Add Chatbots to Your Site

Chatbots have revolutionized the way businesses communicate with clients by providing a faster and efficient mode of communication. This functionality assists in answering questions, offering menu options, and even assists with the customer's order. This type of technology provides convenience to the customer, as they do not have to queue physically to make inquiries. It also reduces the time taken to give feedback to clients

Start Tracking

Tracking helps, you see how your customers are interacting with your site and can help you in increasing your online presence. It is also possible to capture phone IDs and locations, which can be used in customer segmentation. It allows you to measure the results of actions taken on your site.

Using LinkedIn for Keyword Research

This involves using LinkedIn profiles to come up with keyword lists that can be used to enhance search campaigns. Your keywords must clearly state what you offer so that it can link with the target audience. Link your LinkedIn profile to your company page to increase visibility. Think of your LinkedIn company page as your business profile and use it to educate prospective customers more about your company.

The Best Platforms for Your Online Business

There are several social media platforms that one can use to boost their online business. However, without proper understanding and knowledge, this process may be hard, and in some cases, may lead to giving up on social media platforms for marketing.

To avoid this, it is essential to understand how to choose the right social media-marketing platform for your business. To best choose a suitable platform, there are several things one needs to consider.

- Who is your target audience, the various social media platforms appeal to different age groups and thus an essential factor to consider before selecting your platform?
- Find out your objective for using social media marketing; maybe you want to grow your brand. Then a platform such as Facebook will go a long way in achieving this.
- Another way to choose a social media platform for your online business is: Considering your marketing content, if you want to use imagery to increase your sales, then use platforms that specialize in pictures.

- Find out what your competitors are using to boost their sales; this will help in making informed decisions and staying ahead of the game. However, despite studying your competition, always remember to use platforms that best suit you and not because the competitor is using them.
- Finally, how many platforms do you want to use? As mentioned earlier, there are many platforms one can use. However, using all the platforms might now work, and though these platforms have zero or little fees, it is vital to find out, how many sites you will need. This will not only help in saving your money but is a great way to reach your targeted audience.

Now that you have some guidelines on how to choose an excellent platform for your online business, let us look at some popular social media platforms.

Facebook

Studies reveal about a third of the world's population actively uses Facebook every month. This amounts to about 2 billion active users. Making it the most popular and used social media platform for both personal and business uses.

In recent years, the use of Facebook as a marketing tool has increased, and more businesses are using the platform.

Currently, over 60 million businesses, use Facebook for business purposes, out of the 60 million businesses on Facebook about 6 million use Facebook to market their products and services.

Now you may be wondering what makes Facebook so popular? It is simple; Facebook allows users to use various content from videos, texts, to pictures, making it an ideal platform. Another factor that makes Facebook a popular advertising social media platform is the ease in use and entry.

YouTube

This is the second most popular social media platform in the world, with approximately 1.9 billion users monthly. If you specialize in video creation, then YouTube is the platform for you, with users watching about one billion hours of content daily.

Being the second most popular search engine also makes YouTube a perfect platform for businesses. This is due to the high traffic. By using YouTube, you not only get an opportunity to attract potential clients through informative content, but you can also advertise and generate income. YouTube is also a great passive income earner.

Instagram

Instagram is mostly known as a picture sharing application. The app can, however, be used to share short videos, and in recent months Instagram introduced IGTV stories for longer videos. Instagram has over the years gained popularity, and though it was created for personal use, more business owners have managed to use Instagram to boost their businesses.

Instagram now has a business platform where you can keep track of your analytics as well as posts. With an estimated 1 billion active users, Instagram has you converting pictures into sales.

Twitter

A great way to open communications channels, build trust and credibility is by using Twitter, Twitter has about 300 million users, and though used as an advertising tool, and it has gained more popularity as a customer service platform.

For your online business to be a success, it is crucial to build trust, and Twitter does just that, many large and medium companies are using Twitter to receive reactions from their clients. Moreover, since Twitter puts a strong emphasis on real-time information, the response time is faster, in turn improving business.

Additionally, Twitter is used to deliver matters concerning politics, entertainment, or even sports in real-time. For online business owners, you can use Twitter to influence or better yet communicate offers or even gifts to increase your sales.

Pinterest

Just like Instagram, Pinterest is also a picture platform; however, unlike Instagram, Pinterest is mostly used to motivate users to purchase or try out new things. If you want to spread your brand to prospective buyers, then Pinterest is for you. Most online businesses use Pinterest to increase their awareness, which subsequently converts to sales.

In addition, with about 250 million monthly users, Pinterest has been seen to persuade buyers. Research has also revealed that about 78% of the Pinterest users use the platform for inspiration to buy items, making it an excellent persuading business tool.

LinkedIn

Popularly known as a job-searching site, LinkedIn has grown to become a professional site, where people can build their brands, connect with other job seekers and employers. Besides developing a personal name, LinkedIn is also used as a marketing tool. You can now send personalized advertisements to potential clients, or even display ads on the site. Additionally, LinkedIn has in recent years allowed users to create forums and groups where job seekers and employers can discuss matters concerning their industries.

Snapchat

Want to appeal to a younger generation? With about 200 million viewers monthly? Then Snapchat is the way to go, Snapchat is similar to Pinterest and Instagram as it uses pictures and short videos to communicate to users. Initially, Snapchat was used to share between friends, but just like most social media platforms, it is now used as a marketing tool.

Reddit

The final social media marketing platform on our list is Reddit, the good thing about online business is the versatility it offers to business owners, you not only get to market your products, you can also build your brand as a scriptwriter, a life coach, or a tutor and one site that has managed to incorporated many facets in online businesses is Reddit.

Reddit has approximately 300 million active users every month, and the platform allows users to post images, news, ask questions, advertise, or vote on issues. Reddit has several subreddits that enable users to join specific discussions or market their enterprises. For instance, if the subreddit is about writers, then you can send your links, connect with other writers, and even get an opportunity to find out things happening in your industry.

There are many social media platforms used in marketing, but one worth mentioning is Medium. Medium is a publishing platform with the social aspect; users are free to publish and read articles. With about 60 million users, businesses can reach their target audience through informative reads and information. The great thing about Medium is that companies not only get an opportunity to market their products, but service providers also get to showcase their prowess through publishing their articles.

The key thing is finding out what works for your business, use tools that maximize your returns, with just 6 hours weekly you are guaranteed to see improvement in your business. Another vital factor to consider when using social media marketing is quality content. Remember, customers need to see your commitment to providing value. For instance, if you are using Instagram to market your products, invest in a professional photographer. Additionally, take time to find out things happening around you, use new trends that will help your business grow.

Competitor Challenge

Exercise;

- ✓ Spot 2 competitors who are popular in your niche.
- ✓ Spot 2 businesses that are not so popular in your niche.

- ✓ For each, write 3 different things you would like to emulate about their way of branding and marketing.
- ✓ After this, write 3 things you consider as their weaknesses.
- ✓ For the latter, write how you would strengthen those weaknesses to your business' advantage.

Chapter 3: Introduction to Social Media Marketing

Instagram Marketing Tools

Instagram is estimated to have more than half a billion active users. There are many prospective clients on Instagram that you could use to your advantage. It is effortless to sell on the platform because of the large number of potential clients for your products. Regular interactions will lead to proper attention to your products. Marketing your products and involving influencers may be helpful to increase your audience. However, to reach the most massive crowd, you will need to use the Instagram tools available to push your product further. Some of the tools used to market on Instagram are discussed further onwards.

Buffer

It provides an area where you can perform multiple tasks at once and with ease. It allows you to schedule your posts in advance and check how the content you advertise is showing. Buffer makes it easier to manage your account even when you are not interacting with it directly. All you have to do is prepare the posts in advance, set the scheduling on the buffer, and it will post them based on your preferences. However, it is only available for business accounts. It provides free plans and paid plans. The paid plans start from $10 monthly.

Sprout Social

This tool is useful in all sizes of firms and agencies. It provides features for scheduling where you can choose the time or intervals for the publishing of your posts. It also comes with analytical tools that enable you to monitor how your posts are performing on Instagram. The analytics help you to know the kind of content that is preferred by your followers. With this data, you can produce more content that will impress your followers. The data also shows how your competitors are performing. You can gauge your performance based on that of your competitors. It also provides a tool to monitor hashtags and comments. Its cost ranges from $99 to $249 monthly.

Iconosquare

This tool takes an in-depth perspective on performance. It avails you many useful data. It tells you what your followers like, their location, and their influences. This information provided can be used for research purposes to know how you can capture and expand your market quickly. It also has analytics tools to compare your performance to that of your competitors. Its cost ranges from $29 to $59 monthly.

Repost for Instagram

This tool allows you to post photos already posted by your followers or other accounts and then give them credit for the images. Using this tool, you do not have to take new photos; all you have to do is find pictures related to your niche and repost them. It is free since it belongs to Instagram.

Twitter Marketing Tools

Doing the usual tweeting, retweeting, liking, responding to DMs, and interacting with influencers will give you the general organic attention gathered. For you to reach a wider audience, you are going to need to do extra and even spend money. There are Twitter tools created that could help you promote your content on Twitter. Twitter tools help you reach your targeted market easily and makes it easier for influencers to market your content.

Sendible

It is a cross-sectional platform allowing you to manage your accounts on different social media. From Sendible, you can manage all your accounts activities and interactions since all the data is synchronizing in a dashboard. You can create an original post and customize it to fit different platforms. It allows you to access analytics on how your posts are performing. It also shows trending topics in your niche where you can participate in conversations with people who share the same interest as you. It starts with a one-month free trial, and monthly payments are at $29 while annual fees are at $288.

Community.it

It is only available for Twitter. It manages the data on Twitter by breaking it into six sections. The first section shows the mentions concerning your brand. It has an efficient way to show the ones replied and the ones not yet seen. Another part shows your followers. It shows the people who have unfollowed you, influencers and even suggests new followers that you may be interested n based on your previous followers. It shows you the types of influencers in your niche and other major accounts. Another section shows top tweets in your niche. It shows quality content that you can share with your followers. The two different parts allow you to schedule your tweets based on preferences and show analytics of your tweets. It starts with a two weeks free trial. Then a premium follows beginning at $19.99 monthly.

TweetDeck

This tool can be accessed through your Twitter account, downloading a Mac app, or navigating on their site. It started independently, but Twitter now owns it. Its interface is full of columns, which you can customize by yourself. On the columns, you can interact with the mentions and schedule your tweets, messages, and lists to your preference. You can set keywords so that you see all the tweets containing the words.

Further filters can be applied to the tweets you get so you can easily have access to the information you want. It even makes it easier to make your collection of the tweets you like. TweetDeck is free.

Awario

It mainly focused on listening and monitoring patterns on the timeline. This tool allows you to see the mentioning of your brand on different platforms. It also gives you easy access to trending topics in your niche. It makes it easier to spot leads to tweets that may need your products. It also simplifies how you deal with messages and mentions and how you will want to react to them. It allows you to create filters and have access to analytical data. It offers a free trial with inhibitions. The full plan goes for $29 monthly and $290 annually.

Click to Tweet

This tool allows you to easily create links that your customers can use to share tweets related to your brand. They usually have an image and a description. It gives you statistics on the number of people who have clicked on the links. The tool can be used to create the configured tweet and to decide where the link should appear. It is free for five links monthly, and unlimited links cost $4.97 per month or $49.70 annually.

Facebook Marketing Tools

In March of 2016, there as an estimated 1.09 billion people scrolling through the Facebook news feed. That is a lot of traffic that can be used to your advantage as a marketer. Your product might be getting attention from the marketing you have done. However, for you to sell more, you need to be more visible to your market. For you to advertise yourself more, you need to spend money on the campaigns. Some tools go for as little as $5. Some of the marketing tools for Facebook are below.

The Facebook Ads Manager

It is a product of Facebook itself that provides you with the necessary tools you need to use in marketing. Since it is a product of Facebook itself, it has a clear understanding of how targeted advertising works. It is the most basic way of advertising on Facebook. For you to get started, you need to, create, or use a Facebook page that you already had. The page should be the one containing the information you want to promote. You should then choose your target market, and this will help your ad to reach your required audience most shortly and efficiently possible. After making a choice, have a budget set aside for the commercial. It should be accounted for then sit back and wait to see the results of the ad. You can track your results to see how the ad is performing. It is the easiest way to market on Facebook since Facebook itself guides you through it simplifying it ultimately.

Qwaya

It is among the popular ways you can use to advertise on Facebook. The platform is prevalent among media marketers and works in the following methods.

Ads A/B testing. You need to test your ads to know what works best for you so that you do not waste money. Qwaya gives you the ability to test all available variables so that you know what is working best based on your preferences.

Scheduling. When running multiple online advertisements, it becomes harder to track them. With Qwaya, you have a scheduling tool. It enables you to know when your target market is online. Therefore, you can plan on when to run your ads so that they can reach the maximum number of people you are targeting.

Qwaya may not be as simple to understand as Facebook ads, but the convenience that comes with it is worth you spending your time learning how it works.

AdEspresso

It is a very efficient tool to start with, and master and the results obtained from it are remarkable. It is good to deal with large numbers since it provides a clean and accessible analysis of the massive amounts of data it gets. It allows you to customize and see top-performing ads while also showing detailed data that may interest you. It also has an Ad Espresso academy that provides all the answers you may need when you are stuck while dealing with it. The academy also gives you a guide on how to maneuver the tool.

Hootsuite Ads

Hootsuite Ads is a significant platform among social networks due to its ability to schedule updates. It is simple to use, and it comes with the ability to create ads very quickly. It scans your Facebook profile and easily identifies pictures that can you can use in advertisements. It also provides advanced management features to allow you to schedule your ads to meet your target market appropriately.

AdStage

It makes it easy to manage your ads between different platforms by providing a platform where you do not have to manage those ads separately. The rules are automated and give you a chance to schedule your ads based on performances, budgets, and audiences.

Social Media Trends to Apply

Here are a couple of social media trends to apply in 2020:

Chatbots and Messenger Integration

Chatbots are a quick way of providing information. They are mainly for customer service interactions. They help in addressing complaints, solving technical issues, and answering any simple questions that the client may have. In 2020, the advancement in technology is bound to make chatbots more efficient by giving them the ability to interact with customers and provide recommendations. By 2020, it is expected that 80% of mobile users will be using messaging apps as their primary source of communication. Marketers have to conduct their strategies where people are active, and messaging apps are an excellent place to start. More than 100000 companies are using chatbots to communicate with their clients who have direct contact with them. Join the likes of Google, Amazon, and Facebook and incorporate chatbots to your messenger apps to make your marketing strategy more effective.

Social Media TV

Soon social media is expected to replace the TV. With almost everyone consuming their content from YouTube and other streaming platforms, it is possible to eliminate traditional television. TV brands have even started having features that support vertical TV. Vertical TV is increasing in popularity since a more significant number of videos are now recorded on mobile phones. Since social media, television is getting more popular. Advertisers should consider it as a platform to use when marketing their products.

Live Streaming Events

Social media platforms have improved their ability to live stream. It has allowed business owners to show product launches and people to get raw uncut footage. Going live gives prospective customers a chance to know what is happening without them being present in the events. However, being able to participate in the conversations. With research, it is easy for businesses to know what their clients like. Showing them events they would like to be in is a plus because they are more likely to check your account more often. Live streaming is not expensive anymore, by 2020, all you will have to do is use your smartphone to record, and you are ready to go.

Ephemeral Content

It comes in by manipulating people's fear of missing out to your advantage. The content posted only lasts for a short time, mostly 24 hours. Since the information is only out for a limited time, people feel the urge to consume it before it disappears. Using your account to post engaging content frequently will make prospective clients visit your page more often. Since they will not want not to know what is happening. The temporary nature of the material also makes people get comfortable with it because it does not leave a digital copy that is traceable to in the future.

Social Media Listening

Online activity triggers a specific type of ads on your page. The ads that show up coincidentally when you are trying to access a particular kind of information are usually planned ads related to your previous activity online. By 2020, this type of advertising will have grown more since companies use social media listening to know what kind of products are in the highest demand.

Contextual Ads

This type of advertisement is available on websites. They are triggered by keywords to advertise a product related to the information sought after. Contextual advertising helps in focusing more on the target by marketing a product where the individuals are likely interested in them.

Augmented Reality

It allows you to see how a product will fit in your life before you decide to purchase it. Augmented reality technology makes advertising interactive since the customer can see the products and play with them around until they find one that is most suitable for them. Many companies are embracing technology to enhance the customer experience.

Reasons Why Social Media Marketing Works

Now you may be wondering, what makes social media so unique in marketing, read on as we expound on some of the reasons why social media marketing works.

Is Ideal for Start-Up Companies

As earlier mentioned, social media, marketing does not only appeal to large companies but is also an excellent plan for small companies due to low costs. In personal social media pages, your followers are potential clients, thus reaching them becomes easier and faster, additionally creating a business social media is easy and requires little capital.

Allows the Business Owner to Reach a Specific Audience

For more traffic and sales, it is essential to know your target audience. Social media marketing makes it easy to reach these clients. For instance, if you are selling baby products, then marketing your items on mom forums and pages helps increase your sales.

Increases Your Brand Awareness

Social media marketing presents your brand to the world, by providing informative content to your audience; potential customers get to know about your business, in turn increasing familiarity with your company, which then led to more sales.

Helps to Create a Community

Your followers become a community, and this helps gain access to them. Social media communities encourage dialogue among customers and business owners, creating a safe space.

Additionally, social media communities also help businesses identify what your clients want and ways to make their lives even better and this will ultimately cause growth in your business.

Helps Appeal Better to Potential Clients

Using social media as a marketing tool makes clients more receptive to your products or services. Remember, most of the people on social media are connecting with family and friends and finding out things happening around them, making social media, a perfect platform to communicate to people at times least expected.

Improves Your Search Engine Optimization and Website Traffic

A strong social media presence improves your site's credibility and value, in turn, increasing traffic. Additionally, posting videos or other valuable content gives clients a reason to want to find out more about your enterprise. Once in your site, encourage the clients to make either a purchase or subscription to a free service.

Helps the Business Get New Leads through Recommendations

New customers look for online reviews and great reviews help the clients gauge the credibility of the company. Research has also shown customers are likely to buy or seek a service that has positive reviews.

Using social media also helps spread positive reviews through word of mouth to friends and family. The dimensional research revealed positive social media reviews influence 90% of customers.

Another report by the search engine land revealed approximately 70% of clients trust online reviews the same as recommendations from family and friends.

Connects Business Owners and Potential Clients Globally

By using the correct keywords, connecting with famous brands. Social media marketing helps businesses appeal to a larger and newer audience.

Helps to Position Your Business Authoritatively

This works well with service providers as social media allows you to share and communicate with potential clients, in turn, building trust.

Helps Business Owners Increase Their Influence

Once you have built credibility and trust, social media marketing takes it to the next step and increases your influence. Your large audience gains more interest, which can be further turned to sales.

Despite being a great marketing tool, for social media to produce excellent results, it is vital to dedicate time. A report by the hub spot revealed about 80% of business owners, and marketers noted an increase in their traffic after dedicating 6 hours weekly in social media marketing.

Social Media Challenge

Exercise;

- ✓ Note down 3 social media platforms that would work well for your business.
- ✓ Then under each platform, write 3 of the best features you'd use in branding and promotion.

Chapter 4: Business on the Internet

How to Sell Services Online

Selling products and services online does not differ much. The most significant difference is brought by the nature of the business. For example, services can be received via devices, while products need to be physically shipped to the buyer. This factor alters a few aspects of selling but maintains rules of integrity and efficiency in both.

Consider Your Service and Market

For your business to be successful, you need to find a place you will fit in the market. Positioning yourself matters a lot; you are to come up or chose a niche that you are good at and specialize in it. Specializing makes you more suitable for a job. Once you have decided on your niche, you need to do in-depth research so you can fully knowledgeable. You should be able to accurately discuss your area of expertise and answer all the questions that your customers have. Conducting your research and including your experience will position you in your unique place in the market.

Build out Your Website

For this step, you can choose to do it yourself, or you can hire an expert for you. Building a website yourself is not an easy task. You can, however, follow a simple tutorial to create a website based on your preferences for the business. Another option is using a website builder. When using a website builder, all your hosting, domain name and site building are at the same place. It makes your work easier and even allows you to customize your site by just dragging and dropping. Your website should contain all your contact information and how customers can interact with you so they can acquire the service they require. It should also include any other information that your prospective customers may need to boost your sales. It should also have a professional look to build trust with your clients and make your business look credible.

Create the Necessary Pages

For your website to be professional, it has to have some essential pages. The pages give different information and direct the customer, so they can easily find what they want. Some of the pages are as below:

- A home page. It gives the customer a brief but detailed introduction. It tells the services you offer and how you can help them with the services

- A portfolio page. It is a portfolio of your work. It goes into detail to explain previous jobs done and the quality of the services you offer. You can brag at this point and assure your clients on your work ethic

- A testimonial page. It shows reviews that were left by people who needed your services before. Reviews help influence prospective customers since people believe in other people's experiences. Select the best reviews for this page since they are guaranteed to create more sales with ease. However, if your business is starting, it can lack this page. You can publish it once you get some reviews

- A service page. On this page, you go deep into detail on the services you offer. The language used should be clear so that a client understands what you are trying to sell them. Include all the necessary information that the client may have concerning your services. Explain how unique you are and why you are most suited for their needs

- A contact page. On this page, you leave all contacts concerning your business, this can be phone numbers, email addresses, and social media handles. Advise the clients that they can use the connections for any prospective projects

In the end, you will need to figure out how you will be receiving payments. It can be using PayPal or using e-commerce templates. Including all this information on your website makes ready for work.

Generate Traffic and Clients

Services sell more when people visit your site. To increase traffic towards your website, you can use a variety of methods. You can have different blogs where potential clients visit often. On these blogs, post links that lead to your site to attract more traffic. Set up social media accounts. On these accounts, you can give details about your company and advertise your services. You can work with Influencers and affiliates on these platforms. Ensure links leading to your website are available so all traffic can lead to your site. Another way to get clients is by networking and retaining old clients. Old clients stay by offering them quality services. The information provided on the website should be responsible for converting traffic to sales.

Do the Work

After getting clients, you now need to deliver the quality work you promised. Offering your services efficiently and on time builds a reputation, especially for new clients. It also leads to good reviews and maintains previous customers. Following the above steps equips you with all the tools you need to start selling your services.

E-Branding and Selling Products Online

Having a logo, website, and quality products is only the first step to e branding. The essential bit of branding is the correlation between the brand and its customers. Today, millennials become brand fanatics due to influence from popular trends. Therefore, if your products do not seem 'cool' or relate to millennials, who run the internet, then your chances of selling are slim to none. However, how can you brand your products to turn your customers into fanatics?

Quality and Sophistication

Before you launch your business, you already have competitors. Try to be as good as them or better than them. That is the only way to stand out and beat them. Many businesses fear going big because they automatically assume that it will require millions. However, if you can start small, leaving room for growth, then you will manage.

Engage with Them

You can hold competitions, feature your buyers on social media, run polls, and surveys, and conduct discussions to ensure you include your customers in your activities and even in decision-making. When you release a product, ask buyers for their opinion. Make them feel relevant to your brand.

Use Influencer Marketing

As earlier stated, branding is all about relating, and what better way to connect with customers than by collaborating with their favorite public figure. Whether it is a musician, actor, or any local influencer, make consumers feel like you know their preferences.

Efficient Customer Service

Respond to their queries fast and accurately. Train your customer service and sales team to understand your products entirely. This way, they will be able to revert to customers with the correct solution. As your clientele grows, add more customer service representatives to ensure no queuing for long hours.

Do everything you can to show your customers that their opinion matters and that serving them is your priority.

Selling Products Online

At first, things are expected to be slow due to creating and setting up your store. However, as more effort and creativity are put in, an increase in sales is expected. For your products to reach the most people, you will have to increase your advertising platforms. Advertising takes time to show results but with time and putting in the work, every day will provide you with a broader customer base that is satisfied.

Easy Purchase and Great Customer Service

Customers visiting your website tend to have a short attention span. You should, therefore, make it easy to purchase the products you are selling without them overthinking. Obstacles or unclear information is likely to make them overthinking and therefore lose attention to your products. Your site should be easy to maneuver and straightforward.

To make it easier for customers to purchase from your site, you should provide them with confidence. News of bad customer service spreads faster than that of good customer service; to prevent this, make sure you treat your customers well. A sure way of providing confidence to your clients is by offering a refund in case a client is not satisfied.

Secure Your Site

The buying process should be as streamlined as possible to make it easy to make a purchase. Asking for unnecessary information from clients may bum them out and make them lose interest in your products. You should, therefore, only ask for the most important questions to make buying from you easy.

If your site is dealing with the clients' personal information, it is important to have certifications that the site is secure from other trusted sources like McAfee or Symantec. Another option is to have a secure server or have e-commerce services on your site. The shipping of products to clients should be done promptly and make it traceable by the customer.

Create a Great Delivery System

A delivery system entails everything from the cost of delivery, to the delivery options, to the faith the client has that you will deliver. How you present your shipping information on your website and advertisements should give the customer confidence that you are legitimate. It should give clear details on the volumes and finances involved in the shipping and show all the available pickup locations. A flawless delivery system makes sure the clients get their products on time and in good condition. Having satisfied clients is likely to increase conversion rates due to good reviews and keep previous customers coming back to you.

Optimize Your Product Page

For your products to be seen more, they need to be easily found. This can be done by customizing your SEO settings, by adding a title and description and customizing your page URL. Adding descriptions to your images will make them easier to find. When describing your products, you should also use keywords to make them easy to find.

Mobile-Friendly Website

More traffic is coming from mobile users. Your products should be available to all prospective customers surfing the internet. Customizing your website to be available for mobile users will give you access to more customers who may be using their phones when they want to buy your products.

Chapter 5: Forms of Digital Marketing

Affiliate marketing is when a company collaborates with a person or a group of people known as affiliates to increase drive traffic to their website and make sales. Affiliates promote and sell the products online for them to earn a commission. Members can be anyone with a significant social media presence, e.g., bloggers, vloggers, or social media personalities. Influencer marketing, on the other hand, has different priorities. It involves marketing the brand so that a broader audience can understand what it is. Both affiliate marketing and influencer marketing are supposed to increase traffic towards your site and ultimately increase sales.

Track Your Progress

Most programs make it easier to track how your campaign is performing. You can get real-time statistics on the number of times that a link has been clicked to access your site. It is easier to track the number of sales made, impressions, and conversations. From the statistics, it becomes more comfortable to know how your advertisement is performing and the impact it has on the market.

Enhance Promotions

Involving other parties in marketing makes it easier to promote your product to reach a broader market. It makes it easier to create anticipation for your offers. Your customers need to have something to look out for, for example, offers or coupons. Affiliates can be used to create the buzz necessary to keep customers always checking if your company has a suggestion. Members can get discount codes for new products launch or share links towards anything new that may be happening about your company. Sharing promotions with other people make them reach a larger audience, and affiliates can help you with it.

Provide Social Proof

Social proof is people conforming to a kind of behavior because others are conducting themselves the same practice. In the marketing world, this behavior is easily manipulated. People depend on reviews and recommendations to start using new products. When your affiliate marketers give positive reviews for your products. In addition, recommend them to other people it is highly likely for other people who follow them also to take up using the product. The majority of the people tend to search for reviews of products before using them, or others start because they saw a social media personality using them.

Therefore, when your affiliates show off your products, often they are likely to boost the sales to their followers.

Performance-based payments

Affiliates payment is on commission. The commission rates range between 5 percent and 10 percent. Therefore, for them to make money they have to make sales, more sales come with more money. An affiliate marketer can be doing the advertisements without being paid if they are not making sales. It is essential for you since you will know the affiliates to work with more and to concentrate on, based on their transactions. With affiliate marketing, you will receive a return on ad spend (ROAS) of 10:1. It is among the best marketing tactics since it promises visible returns and commission rates are negotiable between you and the affiliates.

Scale Your Online Business.

The team you work with should bring you targeted income. You should, therefore, use all measures to make your team the most efficient in making sales. Bloggers and influencers interact with their followers daily, and thus creating a deal with their followers is an easy task. For affiliates to be more successful, you need to diversify them. Diversifying them will make you reach different audiences and therefore give you more opportunities. You do not want more than a quarter of the affiliate income coming from one source. You should spread the risk so that you are not over-reliant to one affiliate. You should also do your research to know the kind of members working with your competitors. With this kind of information, you can make your working conditions better. In addition, provide a better commission, and you can be sure the affiliates would prefer working with you.

Website Sustainability

Most e-commerce sites fail due to the lack of traffic visiting their sites. Using affiliate marketing is a crucial way to increase traffic accessing your website. Sharing your brand online will make your audience curious, and most of them will visit to check out your brand. Sites have a failure rate of 80 percent, but using affiliate marketing is bound to put you in the successful 20 percent.

Strong ROI

Marketing using affiliates has been seen to increase purchases by order value of clients. It also increases the customer order average and increases the average customer revenue.

Increase Sales.

The strategy has been proven to work with a rising 240 percent. It may be hard to find the perfect affiliates to work with, but once found you can be sure to boost your sales rapidly. It also teaches you how to create and build long-lasting relationships.

Dropship Marketing

Master the Art of Marketing

The dropping business is mostly automated. A decent website, an eye-catching logo, or an even graphically enhanced product advertisement can look quite entertaining. Still, marketing is what puts money into your pockets at the end of the day. To do this, you need to understand how you are going to grow traffic to your website through search engine optimization, learn how to create effective ads, and how to turn your visitors into buyers. Well-crafted ads and search engine optimization will generate more traffic to your website. The more visitors you get, the better the chances of converting a sale. Ads provide short-term sales, while SEO provides sales in the long term through building your rank in searches. Optimized product pages and useful blog content play a key role in acquiring page audience while at the same time maintaining acquisition costs at a minimum.

Post customer reviews, testimonials, and ratings to your site. Potential customers can be skeptical at first regarding the quality of your products. Such shoppers rely on product reviews to make up their minds on a given product. A testimonial can also motivate the shopper to make a purchase.

Create compelling offers. Always put up your products on sale. This motivates people to buy your product, especially when you match a suitable item with an appropriate deal. The same applies to bundle deals. Pay more attention to selling more similar products in the same bundle deal.

Do not underprice your products. To achieve profitability, keep the product cost low and sell the products at the market. Charge more for your product but keep the prices fair to factor in business expenses, cost of goods, marketing costs, and the cost of hiring a marketing team.

Automate your business. Dropshipping tools keep your business automated to give you the luxury of focusing on other interests, such as working on another job. Automation tools will grow your business fast. Other tools exist to post on social media on your behalf while others automate the marketing aspect of your business.

Keep your website, presentable. A customer-friendly website will keep visitors on your site. Visit other websites related to your niche to have an understanding of how to build an effective product page, type of images to use, and the extra features appearing on the websites. Using the Shopify app, create your store in relation to other successful store brands.

Choose the type of store you want. A niche store is different from a general store. A niche store makes finding the proper audience for your products an easy task. Check out similar niche companies before choosing your own to have a more detailed understanding. A general store is for those still experimenting and still trying to find the right niche.

Use Facebook ads to boost your marketing. Facebook boasts of 2 billion users worldwide. Owing to the rich and diverse data it collects, Facebook empowers you to create better and audience-targeted ads. The ads are highly customizable and manageable.

Prepare to adapt. Starting a dropshipping business is relatively easy. However, challenges are still part of the business, and learning how to pivot plays a key role in growing your store. For example, you may be tasked with adding a new trend that falls within your niche to maximize sales. Still, your favorite product may not be the best for your customers, and you may be forced to remove it from the store.

Provide Quality Customer Service. In doing so, you will stand out among your competitors. Offer refunds when necessary, and respond to your customer's queries in a friendly manner to make them feel appreciated and valued. You can even send thank you cards to the returning customer.

Stick to ePacket Shipping. ePacket shipping, other than being cheap, is the most reliable when it comes to delivering products to your customers. Their cheap services allow you to protect your profits when selling products at market value.

Stay active on a daily basis. Like any other business, dropshipping requires effort to grow. Spending at least an hour a day in your business to process customer orders or to respond to inquiries will make you dependable and grow your sales exponentially. Keep the ads running, and make at least one posting on social media each day.

Import a few items when starting. A small collection of goods allows you to launch your dropshipping business swiftly and make sales in no time. It is also much quicker to put up product descriptions for a small number of items. More focus should be put on finding the right product that will provide you with the first sale.

Request product samples. Experience the products you wish to sell first hand. This will help you to come up with suitable product descriptions and take quality pictures of the product.

Use cross-sell and upsell techniques. This marketing strategy assists you to maximize in every transaction. Upsell allows you to suggest to the customer alternative products to boost the mean order value across all orders. Cross-sell empowers you to merge products that befit a given product bundle.

Create a blog to drive traffic to your business. Apart from being a cheap marketing strategy, blogs empower you to drive traffic to your site, build an audience, and sales all at ago. In SEO, good blog entries translate to better ranking of your website, too, on the search results page.

Introduction to Email Marketing

Creating an email list to keep in touch with your customers is one of the most effective ways of marketing and remarketing in the digital world. An email list is a directory holding all customer and subscriber emails in one database. These emails are collected via a pop-up message set up on your website and linked to your email list. While these seem technical and complex, SaaS (software as a service) companies have simplified it for everyone by creating email database software that is set up in just a few minutes.

A few decades ago, companies would need to type out emails to their vast clientele one by one. Even with the help of Microsoft's mail merge feature, sending out emails was not so personalized, and not an easy task. The greatest hustle that SaaS companies eliminated was the manual typing of each client's email address to the emailing system. Today, once a client types out their address, the system picks it up automatically.

How Email Marketing Works

As a business, you may want to use your email lists to send out newsletters, offers, survey your customers, product upgrades and such as information to keep your clientele updated and actively involved. You can also create several lists that send different information to different clients.

For example:

If you want to run a one-month campaign and during that campaign, you will give clients some sort of assignments and get feedback. Few weeks before the campaign begins, you may advertise the upcoming activity using your website's pop up feature and let those interested in participating, join in by submitting their email addresses. Now, you can use the standard company email list to inform everyone of the campaign, but provide a link that redirects him or her to submit his or her emails for the campaign. This campaign list will only last until the campaign is done. After this, you cannot email the subscribers regarding other non-related information or activities.

As with the above example, you can conclude that one company can have as many email lists as possible. In addition, you can separate your clients in the database in terms of your category audiences. However, to avoid doubling your work and losing some valuable clients in the midst of it all, it is advisable to have one email list. If you launch a new campaign, just involve everyone in your standard list to avoid confusion as well.

Therefore, email marketing is the process of collecting emails from customers and interested parties to use them - in the future - to sell and resell your products and services. To sort your email marketing, you need at least two tools:

- An email marketing software
- A website pop up software

Note that both these tools can be custom made (programmed) for your company. However, new businesses (startups) can get efficient and free services of both online.

How often should you send emails?

While there is no standard rule for this, it is advisable to send at least one email per week to your clients. Just like with social media marketing, you do not want to spam clients, but at the same time, you do not want them to forget your existence. Therefore, find a balance; hence, once, or twice a week is reasonable.

Do not email your clients every time a staff member sneezes. Make your email count by capturing only important features of your business. As mentioned, you can inform clients about upcoming or ongoing offers and discounts. That is worth an email. If new products are in, let your clients know. If a new service is in beta mode, tell your clients to take it on a test drive and give you feedback.

Sending out irrelevant information might cause clients to unsubscribe or spam your emails. Speaking of spamming, did you know that there are laws governing email communication? Yes, policies have been put in place to ensure client rights are practiced.

Do Not Subscribe a Client Without Their Consent

A newsletter subscription can only be approved by the subscriber. It is illegal to add emails to a list without prior consent from the address owners.

Every Email Sent out Must Contain the "Unsubscribe" Button

A subscription may end up being rather *useless* to the email owner after some time. Say, they wanted to get a one-time service; they received it, we are happy, but no longer needs information from you - the service provider. This client has the right to unsubscribe to your company's newsletters. The presence of the 'unsubscribe' button and page ensures this process occurs in a quick and fruitful way. Allowing unsubscriptions is a magnificent way of reducing spam in emails. You will also be able to only reach a relevant crowd. Newsletter companies charge for this software service per the number of emails subscribed. Those not interested will save you a bunch of money by unsubscribing as well.

Creating the Pop-Up Message

As mentioned earlier, the pop-up box is designed for the website to collect emails from new readers of the website. A doormat appears in the first few seconds of being on a web page. This box can be used to either welcome readers and offer them newsletter subscription opportunity, or use to advertise a new product, eBook, workshop, etc. that a reader may be interested in buying or enrolling.

Have a list of all critical aspects you need to capture in your message. Come up with a design and decide on the best template to be used while building it. A pop-up box becomes ten times more effective when placed in the middle of the site/screen. When set at the bottom side corners, it can be easily missed by the reader. In addition, when placed at the top side corners, one may shrug off as unnecessary browser info. If you place it as a part widget on the browser, a reader might miss it in case they do not scroll all the way to see it. Therefore, place it at the center; the message is clear and to their face. They will definitely read a word or two before clicking the cancel button, and a word (the right word) is enough to make them change their mind and hit *subscribe.*

Either way, a pop-up box has one end game - to collect emails.

Every pop-up box should be brief and to the point, as well as attractive or entertaining with its copy. A pop-up box can contain brief text, images, or both. If you are selling an eBook, it is best to have an image of the book's front cover alongside text that entices the reader to download. This, however, does not mean that pop-ups without images do not convert - they definitely do. All that matters is the text and how convincing you sound.

Just like the emails, you send out, your pop-up box should have an *opt-out* option. This can either be the symbol "X" at the upper right corner or a button beside the subscribe button that says "No Thanks," "Cancel," or something similar.

Yes, a pop-up box should appear in the first five seconds of a reader's time. It can also appear when a reader first scrolls the page. Another way to set it up is having it pop up when a reader is trying to leave the website. This ensures that whether or not they got what they were looking for, they can still leave their email for future purchases.

With all that said, take note that your website's pop up box is the first step to converting a prospect into a customer. Pop-ups work best when they come with an offer for subscribing so do not shy off 'bribing' your readers a little bit. A good pop up also requests for at least the first name of the prospect alongside the email. This way, all emails sent to them can address them by name and feel more personalized.

Sending Newsletters

After subscribing, a prospect expects to receive useful information about your products or services. Unfortunately, sometimes the corporate emails arrive in the spam folder. Therefore, it is important to have a message at the end of a subscription that instructs the subscriber to move your email from the spam or junk folder to the primary inbox.

Almost no one on earth checks his or her spam folders. Hence why you do not want your email marketing efforts to be in vain. You can have a welcome email sent to them so that they can use it to move the email.

The welcome email is your opportunity to impress and build a relationship with your client. Based on the nature of your brand, it should be able to initiate subscriber engagement. It should also introduce your brand, offer contact details; talk about what the newsletters will entail and have a link to your social media platforms. Keep the email simple and short and use a natural tone.

You can also include links back to your website to complete the conversion process. Your welcome email should provide more info that will trigger the prospect to make a purchase. You may include a call to action to help fulfill that purpose.

Types of Email List Software

There are a couple of email newsletter providers (SaaS companies) that offer the service from free to premium packages. The most common ones include:

- MailChimp
- Constant Contact
- Benchmark Email
- HubSpot
- Active Campaign
- Vertical response

- Sendible
- Streamsend
- Sendlane
- AWeber
- GetResponse

Email marketing is very effective in that you get to personally inform a prospect of an offer or related brand activity. Using appealing email subjects would mean more clicks into your emails. Using brief but detailed and also appealing email messages and links will also increase your rate of clicks into your website.

Online PR

It is the process of influencing your products to online users. It involves the use of social media platforms, news channels, forums, and communities to create a conversation about your products. It enables the brand to reach a broader audience than it would usually be impossible to achieve with traditional public relations. Online presence of a product allows for interaction with the customers and get feedback concerning the same. It enables us to focus on the target market and to spread more information concerning the product at a quicker rate.

Differences between Online and Traditional PR

Traditional PR is when the advertisers collaborate with journalists so they can feature in printed media, radio, and television. Online PR, however, is campaigning on the internet and by word of mouth. Traditional PR is different from Online PR in the following ways:

- The channels used. Traditional PR uses press media. Press media is newspapers, magazines, radio, and television. Online PR mainly depends on social media and websites to as share information

- Message conveyed. In traditional PR, companies share their data with uninterested customers. Mostly they showed their progress and gave irrelevant information out there to customers they were not even sure were ready to consume their content. They were sharing their stories with uninterested listeners. In online PR, it is the other way around. Branding is essential in online PR. Influencers have to come up with creative content to attract customers. Influencers have a target market, and they, therefore, have to come up with quality and valuable content so that they can retain the followers an keep them excited about the content

- Formats used in PR. Traditional methods involved journalists who spread the information through press releases and articles. In the modern world, there has to be a conversation. Conversations happen on social media, blogs or even multimedia. It makes people interact more so the result of the information shared can be easily acquired

- The tone used to market the products. In traditional methods, companies used a formal tone. It was straightforward to know business-related content from regular content. Nowadays, most brands have adopted an informal way of communicating with their customers. The sound of their conversations is friendlier, which helps to show the human side of the brand. Intimate discussions make it easier to interact with their customers and influences more as compared to the commanding formal tone

- Tools used. In the past, influencers used large spreadsheets that contained large amounts of contact information they could use to send data from messages to Gmail, Outlook, and Yahoo. Nowadays, we deal with the CRM (Customer Relationship Management), which integrates all the company's contact information and manages it. It makes it easier to share information as compared to the traditional methods of copying and pasting

The above are just some of the comparisons evident between the traditional and modern forms of PR. However, modern ways have come to make it easier to conduct relationships and made them more useful.

What Does Digital PR Involve?

Digital PR involves combining both traditional methods and modern trends to ensure the product reaches as many people as possible. They market the brand as ambassadors churning out the best content they can for the brand. Content creators create relationships with other influential individuals by mentioning them or linking to their websites to reach as many individuals as possible. Influencers release the information with the relevant links to direct the clients to your site.

The Goal of Digital PR

The main objective of PR is to ensure more visibility of the product. It also makes a better impression of the brand to its customers. Digital PR aims to beat the competitor by having a superior brand using all the available digital tools. Superiority will make them more visible in the majority of the online audience and make it the brand of choice. The goal is to beat competition among rivals. You should also have a space in the large pool of available audience, and this is achieved by conveying helpful information to your customers and providing solutions for their problems.

How Digital PR Can Benefit Your Brand

A proper online campaign can be beneficial for your brand. It helps in improving the company image by allowing it to interact with its customers and improving. It increases traffic to your site since the information reaches a broader audience, and therefore more people will visit the website. More substantial traffic is bound to increase more sales or leads since many people will interact with the website.

Repurpose Your Content

Already written content can be modified so that it is suitable for digital marketing. Extra information can be added to the existing data to provide more information or make it more user-friendly. A short video or a LinkedIn update can be incorporated to provide further information concerning the brand.

The Difference Between Online PR and Marketing

Marketing is mainly about the number of sales that you can acquire. It involves promoting a brand directly to increase its success rate in the market. Online PR refers to creativity around the product. It shows how unique the product is and spreading awareness about the product. It aims at building relationships while also promoting the brand. Marketing goes hand in hand with PR for the brand to be successful, and this is because links must exist for sales to happen.

Get Started with a Digital PR Campaign

You can choose to do it yourself or higher a firm to do it for you. Having a clear target of your goals and objectives, then enhancing the power of the internet is bound to bring success to your brand. Embrace all the feedback and act on it accordingly to provide services that are suitable for your target market.

Inbound Marketing

In recent years, marketing strategies have evolved to suit various needs and time, and one factor that has contributed significantly to this change in marketing is the use of the internet.

There are various marketing methods, but before settling on one, it is vital to understand your audience and the cost. Now let us look at inbound marketing and some of the advantages you incur from using this method.

Inbound marketing is a marketing strategy that seeks to attract potential clients by using content marketing at different stages of a sale to generate more sales. This is contrary to outbound marketing, which presents a brand, service, or products to prospective clients in the hope of generating sales.

Inbound marketing works by attracting and engaging visitors through search engine optimization techniques, use of social media, blogs, YouTube channels, or even a website.

Difference Between Inbound Marketing and Outbound Marketing

Inbound marketing, as mentioned earlier, seeks to engage potential customers through content marketing. For instance, if you have a blog, you can write informative content for your visitors but include a call to action. This, in turn, may generate sales.

Another way inbound marketing, appeals to people is through earned media; this may be through hashtags, discussion forums, features on news platforms. Earned media, as the name suggests, comes by because of your work and performance in the business.

Outbound marketing, on the other hand, mostly relies on traditional means to reach the target audience. These may be through newspaper advertisements, magazine features, and paid social media advertisements to mention a few.

Now that you know the difference, what are some of the advantages of considering inbound marketing?

Helps to Reach Organic Audience.

Inbound marketing helps to reach quality visitors. These are visitors likely to purchase or seek your services in turning reducing costs on un-necessary marketing.

Increases Credibility

Remember, the targeted audience gets attracted to your site, or blog or YouTube channel because you offered valuable information. This approach has been seen to increase trust among buyers and sellers as the clients feel you are reliable.

Offers a Variety of Marketing Plans

These marketing platforms are attained at zero or a small fee, making it an ideal marketing plan for both large and small businesses. You not only use your blog to reach clients, but you can also use referrals from your website or even social media pages.

Inbound Marketing Is a Long-Term Marketing Plan

If you are in business for a short time, then inbound marketing may not work for you. However, if you are in for the long haul, inbound marketing is the plan for you. Inbound marketing though requires time and patience to pay off in the end.

Provides Analysis and Measurements

Inbound marketing helps generate analysis on how a business is fairing. By using Google analytics you can see how many people visited your site, or blog, and from which part of the world. This, in turn, helps in making informed changes in the business.

How to Get Started with Inbound Marketing

For inbound marketing to be a success, it is essential to pay attention to your content. You need to create content that captures, engages, and provides value to prospective clients. However, before you start using inbound marketing, here are a few pointers to follow.

- Know your target audience.
- Know your voice to you stand out in inbound marketing you need to be authentic.
- The third tip is choosing your marketing platform.
- Finally, after creating your content, present it to the world, have a schedule. For instance, if your platform is YouTube, then you may schedule your videos for Thursday; this helps to increase your traffic subsequently more sales.

Once you have initiated your inbound marketing strategy, one tip to help you stand out is creating fresh content every time. Remember, the potential clients will buy your products if you offer new information, so always be the first to inform them.

For inbound marketing to increase and generate sales, it is crucial to stay relevant, informative, and patient. As previously mentioned, inbound marketing is a long-term marketing tool, and though it may take time before you make huge sales, with the right approach you are bound to see changes in your business.

Pay-Per-Click (PPC) Marketing

PPC is an acronym for Pay per Click. It is an online advertising strategy where you pay publishers to advertise on their platforms. In search engines such as Google and Bing, advertisers bid on key phrases that face higher traffic on search engines. When such phrases appear the search, their ad will also appear, therefore marketing it. Some websites, however, usually offer a flat rate for all advertising and got rid of the bidding process. PPC can be in the form of words, where the advertisement shows in text form. It can be in the form of a banner or display that has pictures and explains more on the product advertised. The ads are targeting to increase more traffic to the sites they are selling. More clicks mean more payments made by the advertisers.

Benefits of PPC

The main advantage of using PPC is to increase traffic to your desired destination. However, you may be asking yourself just how different it is as compared to other forms of advertising. Read on as we analyze further benefits of using PPC:

PPC is measurable and easy to track. There is no mystery when it comes to PPC. Clicks can easily be tracked and calculated in an advertisement using Google analytics. From this, it is easier to see how a campaign is performing.

Easier to get into the market. With the right strategy and positioning of your campaign, you can quickly get into the competitive market. All you have to do is to set up the advertisement. PPC enables you to reach your target market easily rather than just casting your net blindly. The ads are placed strategically for people who may be interested in your product.

You are in total control. With PPC, you have full control based on what you want. You can start small and grow as time goes according to your budget, stop as soon as you wish and you get to choose where to place your ad based on the keywords and phrases that you prefer.

It has incredible targeting options. You have a variety of choices you can make on advertising. The choices range from the keywords you choose, device, location to even the time you want the advertisement to show. The options help you to customize your ads to reach your target market in the easiest way possible.

It is easily compatible with other methods of marketing. Since it is online, it is easier to combine it with other forms of marketing that you use. PPC works well with SEO strategy, which you can use to see the number of impressions that a campaign that you put forward has generated.

Main PPC Platforms

PPC marketing is available in a variety of sites. Some of the common platforms for PPC marketing are listed below:

- Google AdWords
- Bing
- Yahoo

- Facebook

- Advertising.com

- Bidvertiser

- Revcontent

The above named are just a few of the sites where PPC is available. They are, however, used in any websites with a high rate of traffic.

Remarketing

It is a common practice used by advertisers to retarget for attention. It happens when someone visits a site but does not perform the desired task on their website. Therefore when visiting another different website, an advertisement may pop up that is selling the product from their website. The ads usually contain pictures of the products to attract the visitor back to their site.

Traffic

Online traffic is the amount of data transacted by visitors. It mainly shows the number of people who visited the site and how long they spent on it. Websites use this data to know how popular they are and which parts of their blogs interest people the most. Traffic to a site influences how much advertising can be on the site. Websites with higher traffic have more advertisements because people will want to direct some of the traffic to their sites. More traffic to a place leads to more success since it means the information is reaching a more significant number of people.

PPC with Google

Directing traffic to your site is not as easy as it seems. Google PPC comes in handy to help you achieve your desired traffic. People looking for items you are selling can find you easier based on their searches. Your advertisements are strategically placed to reach your target market easily. It is because the words they use to search for the content trigger the choice of adverts they are likely to see.

Video Marketing

Since 2014, visual content marketing has become one of the most popular digital marketing methods. This is because prospects do not just hear about your service or product; they experience it visually making it more real for them. Video marketing is the art of using product and service explained clips to inform prospects of what they are about to purchase.

Using videos has also been a good way to eliminate long product manuals that most people never understand anyway.

Why You Should Use Video When Marketing Your Brand

The use of videos is quite entertaining and easy to understand, and with millennials getting more disinterested in reading lengthy texts, a simple explanatory video will go a long way. Videos, however, have been proven more effective for products (including software), than services. Picture seeing a nice handbag image on some e-commerce site. Now, picture seeing a video of the same handbag but by a different seller. If this video shows how the handbag looks from all angles and shows inside pockets and other amazing features, then this seller has a 100% upper hand over the image seller.

This image means that you will get what you get and all you can do is hope. However, the video means you will get what you have seen. So no surprises on arrival. In addition, videos tend to be accurate on materials and such features of products. Some images may not show exact material due to editing, lighting, and camera quality. Others may be a fake version of a popular material but as a buyer, you may not tell. With a video, however, everything becomes known. You will be able to see exactly how a product is and how it works. Therefore, if you would prefer a video to images and text, then so will your customers.

Types of Videos

There are different types of videos that you can apply when marketing. Pick the one that fits your type of campaign and relates to your audience. Below are a few types:

Product explainer video. They are all about explaining how and why a product works, including the problem it solves and reasons for buying it. Showing viewers the effectiveness of a product is giving them a reason to buy. These are also good for services.

Demo videos. This video captures a product in action. If it is a vegetable cutter, you cut up vegetables to show the effectiveness of the tool. This helps a viewer decide if that is the type of gadget, they want.

Brand and culture videos. They give your audience information about your brand helping with general build awareness.

Case study videos. It is always important to put a product or service into some sort of experiment before launching it to see if it provides the targeted solution. This is called a case study. During a case study, you may choose to record the process as evidence of the experiment. When a prospect sees the product or service working for other people, they will not hesitate to buy.

Interview videos. As the brand owner, you can organize for some interviews where you will talk about your product or service and just create awareness of them. Let people know your reasons for creating that item, let them relate with you and get a reason to promote you buy purchasing. Appeal to their emotions.

Teaser videos. Everyone loves some suspense, and just like a movie trailer, you can get entertaining by teasing your product or service. Talk about a few awesome features and how they work, then leave everyone in suspense and give them a purchase link.

Creating a Video Marketing Strategy

Creating a video marketing strategy is essential for any business because every step needs a calculated plan to succeed. Just like every other strategy, a video marketing strategy starts with knowing your goals and objectives. What are you trying to achieve with this video? Could it be driving traffic to your site, getting people to subscribe to your newsletter, or influencing someone to make a purchase or enroll for training? Whatever your reasons, understand them, understand your audience, and pick the type that works best.

After, select the preferred channel for your video. Where will the video be posted? This is answered by where you are trying to capture your audience. If you are looking to grab YouTube viewers, you can create a YouTube channel and post the video there. If you want it on your website only, you can use video players like Vimeo to achieve that.

The next step in your strategy is about timelines. When do you want to launch the video online? This factor will affect a few things including the duration available for video production. If the video needs to be out in a week, a demo video might be more effective. Keep in mind the stages of video production:

- Setting up the presentation and venue
- Taking the video
- Reviewing and editing the video

While these steps seem few and easy to do, some videos (depending on the type and length), might require even a month to complete. Therefore, know what your video type entails, and plan for a more reasonable timeline. In the process, learn how much you will need for the production and editing and get what you can afford. However, remember the video must be of high quality; therefore, you may need to squeeze your pocket a bit.

Finally, have a launch strategy and how you will share the video on social media. With your set targets, you can review the video performance and impact at the end of your marketing campaign.

Types of Video Distribution Channels

Some of the best channels for your video include:

- Website
- Social Media
- YouTube
- Messaging app shares
- Landing pages
- Emails, etc.

Before getting a study with video marketing, check your analytics. This will make it easier for you to spot progress with your upcoming videos.

Mobile App Marketing

Here are a few reasons why you should have a mobile app for your business:

Stay Ahead of Your Competition

A mobile app not only helps to showcase your products or services to customers but is also a great marketing tool, by ensuring you reach your clients at their convenience. A study done in 2016 revealed that around 62% of businesses have a mobile application, and this number continues to increase by the day.

Showcase Products

Mobile applications have been seen to ease the customer's experience by ensuring products are on display and easily accessible. Additionally, a business mobile application gives the business the freedom to showcase new products on sale, in turn, increase sales.

Push Notifications

Push notifications are an essential communication and marketing tool in any business, with a mobile app, companies can inform their customers on new deals or even advertise new products. This is an effective way to ensure the customers receive important notifications.

New Audience and Customer Prefer Using Mobile Phones

A mobile phone is one of the most used and popular gadgets in this tech era, with millennials spending about 90 hours each month in smartphone applications. Having a mobile app thus allows the business to reach a wider audience, additionally, since smartphones are easy to use, yet updated. More people prefer accessing services through their phones, making mobile applications an ideal growth opportunity for businesses.

Cultivate Customer Loyalty

With the many advertisements on digital platforms, customers may lack a connection with a specific brand. To prevent this, consider using a mobile app for your business, a mobile app will not only help the clients access your products and services faster but creates a connection through the fast and reliable communication channels, in turn cultivating loyalty.

How to Market Your Mobile App

Create a landing page with the app download link
Make your first impression informative and creative by using landing pages, also known as lead capture pages. Your mobile application lead capture pages should include the app name

and features, informative promotion video, and a call to action.

Note: Ensure the call to action is clear on what you want clients to do.

Make Your App Visible in App Stores

For a mobile application to be visible on the app store, it is crucial to rank high on searches. This subsequently leads to an increase in prospects, factors that affect an application's visibility include:

- Your logo or icon, make use of a logo that represents your brand and is unique.
- Description, let people know what gap your mobile app intends to fill; additionally, include keywords.
- Title, make the title, short, and easy to understand; this ensures clients can easily remember your app's name, in turn increasing downloads, which subsequently increases sales.
- Include screenshots; for your app to be visible in searches, it is essential to show the clients features to expect, and an easy way to gain trust and credibility is by using pictures.

Measure Your App KPI

Finding out how your mobile application is fairing in the market will help you make informed marketing decisions. Thus important to regularly analyze your app's key performance indicators (KPIs), your app KPI enables you to keep track of daily downloads, daily and monthly active users, retention rate, these are the number of users who come back to the application after downloading and finally KPIs helps app developers to find out the number of people who stopped using the app.

Market Early

You do not have to wait until the mobile app is ready to present it to the world, consider creating development videos on the app's progress, and incorporate surveys and polls to find out what your potential customers think about your application. Marketing your mobile app early is a great way to influence action and spark communication with potential clients.

Get Reviews

Research has revealed that about 84% of customers depend on reviews to determine a brand's credibility. On the other hand, around 68% of prospects form an opinion on a service provider or even a mobile app after reading the reviews. Thus, an essential part of marketing your app encourages your customers to share their experiences with your mobile app.

Social Media and Influencers

Make use of social media platforms to spark discussions about your app; social platforms such as Twitter are especially useful in creating hashtags. These discussions increase your app's popularity, in turn, increasing the number of users. Another method to raise awareness on your app is by using influencers, for instance working with a popular actor to present your mobile app in the market will help build credibility in the app.

Chapter 6: Content Creation and Marketing

Advertisements have evolved from newspapers to social media marketing and branded content. Traditional marketing styles are becoming less popular by the day, and although social media marketing has a lead in the marketing world, one arising issue is the use of pop-up advertisements.

Now users have resorted to blocking the advertisements, which means poor sales for businesses, to pass across a message but still stay relevant on content, businesses have now resorted to branded content.

Read on to get a better understanding of branded content and go through some of the advantages of branded content as well as get a more in-depth understanding of traditional marketing and branded content.

What is Branded Content?

Branded content influences the creation of material that closely touches their brand, and this allows the reader or viewer to make the connection. Branded content marketing aims at influencing discussion around the brand.

Additionally branded content marketing, aims at providing value to their clients, rather than generating sales. The discussions help in building the credibility of a brand, which later on increases the sales. Moreover, content created will not only tick your curiosity about a brand but will also entertain you.

Branded content is not limited to one format. On the contrary, content creators are open to using games, videos, interviews, or podcasts.

Differences Between Branded Content and Other Marketing Strategies

- Unlike other types of marketing that pay close attention to a product or services, branded content subtly provides brand information. Allowing the buyer to focus on other aspects of the brand.
- Open for voluntary participation, be it through reading an article or watching an exciting video or by just playing a game. This is different from other types of marketing that add pop-up ads on the screen. These pop-up advertisements may be invasive, which may later lead to a decrease in sales.
- Branded content allows content creators to take control, for instance, if a brand will feature in a script. Then it is the creator's job to place the brand in the script.

- Another major difference is product placement of the brand; conventional marketing strategies solely focus on the brand and create their content around the brand. Branded content, on the other hand, may be present in content or not. Making the sole focus of branded content an opportunity to understand a brand.

Advantages of Branded Content

- Besides allowing voluntary participation, branded content creates an emotional connection. In some cases, branded content makes use of stories about their companies, which makes customers feel part of a community, subsequently increasing sales.

Developing an Emotional Attachment Takes You to the Next Advantage.

- Branded content improves credibility and trust between businesses and prospective clients by helping buyers understand their brands better.
- Increases customer loyalty, customers become loyal to a brand they understand and trust, making branded content an ideal marketing strategy. Loyal clients mean repeat clients and positive reviews, which contribute significantly to the success of any business.

- Increase the ability to influence, the positive association linked with your brand, increase the ability to spark action.
- Branded content increases brand awareness; from the stories and interactions, the users understand your voice as a brand.
- Increases traffic, though branded content aims at creating a connection by providing value. This technique has been seen to increase traffic. However, it is important to note; branded content will not increase your traffic in a day, nor a week. It is essential to put in the time to strengthen the relationship between the customers and your brand.

Brands That Have Successfully Used Branded Content

One of the top companies around the world that have managed to stand out is Coca-Cola. For years, Coca-Cola has used stories to help customers understand them better. This marketing method has made it one of the most successful and influential brand globally.

Another brand that has successfully increased traffic from branded content is Bloomberg. Bloomberg uses an inclusion blog to connect with more clients. The blog provides information on leadership and finances, putting the company on top of the game.

Proper marketing plays a big part in a company's success and for a long-term marketing strategy, and then using branded content is the way to go. Branded content not only leaves a mark in people's lives but also puts your brand on the leading board.

Content Writing for Brand Building

There are several types of content writing used to build a brand's online presence. They include, but are not limited to:

- Blog posts
- Social media copy
- Post captions
- Web page copy
- Landing page sales copy

All the above are used for marketing a brand online. When it comes to content, we focus on two aspects; copywriting and search engine optimization.

What is Copywriting?

Copywriting is the art of writing text to influence/convincing the reader to take a particular action. This selling text is referred to as a *copy*.

Copywriting is one of the most powerful brand-building tools from centuries back. It has all about making consumers *relate* to your brand. Unfortunately, writing copy is not an 'everybody-skill' some train for it, and some are just gifted with it. The point is, before attaching any copy to your brand, hire a professional copywriter to either write it or edit it.

When dealing with online platforms, it is crucial to consider all texts that talk about your brand as a copy. Meaning the writings on your home page and the captions on social media should be written by a copywriter or with the copywriting aspect in mind.

Copywriting is also done on advertisements. The text you read that makes you laugh and purchase, agree and purchase, feel some emotion and make a purchase that is a copy. A copy intends to make your customers relate and make a move.

Now, it does not always have to be a purchase. Sometimes you may want consumers to follow you on social media, share a blog post, sign up to your newsletter, or download an item online. Whatever action you want them to take; they do it because your copy convinced them. Video marketing also applies copy in the voice over. Yes, it is spoken but from a written script. That script is a copy, and it will be the reason for the purchase.

What is SEO?

Search engine optimization is attempting to double website traffic by ranking highly on search engines. To rank high, a website would need a few things including;

- Quality content
- External links to authoritative sites
- Internal links to performing posts
- Use of long-tail keywords
- Use of images and graphs

How Does SEO Come in Content Writing?

In the tips above, you will notice that all those can only be applied in content. Industry keywords can be used on web copy and blog posts. Links are mainly applied to blog posts. Images and graphs can be used on all platforms.

SEO can also be applied to a copy, which is termed as SEO copywriting, where your copy ranks on search engines as well.

Chapter 7: Enabling Your Sales Team

This handbook is dedicated to talking about marketing as one of the golden tools of lead generation. This makes your sales team the 'prized possession.' As they directly interact with consumers interested in your products, they hold the key to better sales and profit margins. This means that these individuals should be well equipped with the information and skills to convert a prospect into a buyer. They should also be tech-savvy and up to date with technology and business trends in your industry. Therefore, how can you enable your sales team?

Provide Training

When you hire members of your sales team, you need to train them about your products intensively. Let them know your business policies and terms of sale. This training should include nitty details like how to pronounce a product to its features and costs. If they cannot sell in their sleep, then they are not equipped with enough information.

Keep Them in the Loop

Do not make the mistake of releasing a new product or product update without informing your sales team first. Weeks before launch, it is recommended to conduct product training with your sales team. Tell them about the new product and why you are incorporating it into your inventory. If it is an update, teach them about the new features they have and what makes them better than the older versions. Keep your sales team in the loop with every release and release date.

Reference a Script

Depending on how many products or services your business offers, keep in mind that your sales team is made of humans and not computers. If your business has a vast inventory, these humans may not be in a position to remember them all with their features and prices. This is where a product information document comes in handy. For instance, if a customer inquiries about a specific product, the sales team member can reference the script and give accurate information. Ensure this 'script' is always updated with new product information.

Create a Sales Playbook for Them

This is mostly for your newbies. Every company has the factors that make it sell. A way in which they land those customers faster and make a good profit. A season of high yields and how to maximize them. Create a sales playbook for your team. Let your sales team know the strengths and weaknesses of your company and products. Let them in competitor information and how to use to their advantage – without tarnishing any brand. Give them the dos and don'ts in the playbook so that they can maintain a similar script ad consistency in their work.

Understanding Customer Intent

Customer intent is the reason behind a purchase. What is the intention of purchasing a particular product? Once you know the intentions of your customers, you can influence their buying. Unlike physical stores, it is a bit of a challenge to understand what a customer is looking for when they start browsing. However, once they get to your website, you can tell where their interests lie if they are looking to purchase that product or service.

When it comes to customer preference, you look at specifics on what they prefer. A bunch of customers may intend to purchase mobile phones from your store, but not all will purchase iPhones. Different people pick different items depending on personal preference. Preference is never really about the item; it is more about the *type* of item. Is it big or small, heavy, or light, black, or red, slender, or broad? This is why to achieve more sales, you are recommended to have a variety on each category to quench different preferences.

Artificial intelligence-powered tools have been developed to monitor buyer activity/behavior to conclude their 'intent' and provide options as they browse on different platforms. Invest in AI eCommerce tools such as cookies.

You see how you browse a particular web page, and ever since, keep seeing ads on that product or service? That is the magic of cookies and Google remarketing. Other platforms like Facebook do that, as well. When you add cookies on your website for your customers, it increases the chances of purchase.

Chapter 8: Developing Your Brand Experience

Brand experience refers to experiential marketing, which incorporates various sets of conditions formed by an organization to influence its consumer's feelings regarding a product. Using a combination of different modes that a consumer applies when interacting with a brand, different companies try to form an atmosphere of goodwill and dependability between the brand as well as a specific demand.

With that said, the brand experience offered to clients matters. If the consumers are engaged with the product, they shall send more clients your way. They will also highly recommend you to others. On the other hand, if they have the appalling experience, they shall share with their contacts, thereby leading to a disastrous financial consequence. Since customers are selective in choosing the person they would like to be in business with, providing an impeccable brand experience is by no means, no brainer. Here are some of the tips you can use to create an impressive brand experience for your business.

Create Fluid Content

Your clients live busy lives. They are also often on the go. For that reason, they keep changing devices to get the products they want quickly. At the same time, they would like to gain access to these products anytime they please. Because their choices keep expanding progressively, approximately 4 million consumers are connected to new smart devices.

For a business professional in the field of marketing, this implies that you must captivate your targeted audiences while supporting your current users. That way, you will be in a position to garner new clients. To improve your chances of wooing more clients into your business, you should focus on improving the site. This will provide a better user experience.

Build a Fluid and Dynamic Media

Not long ago, business professionals and marketers alike would set their yearly media plans in stone. Would they not only research and plan but also execute their ideas using a radio. Today, it is precarious to form a strategy that will remain dormant for about 8 months. Therefore, entrepreneurs need to invest in modern media since it is strategic and fluid. This implies that you may use various distribution channels as well as shifts entirely based on receiving actual results.

Here, you can easily create a personalized video for your clients using a contact list exported from Google. The file should have at least three columns, including the client's name and email. It is also essential to append every consumer's first name into the list.

Incorporate Swag

In the real sense, a business should be a profit-generating venture. Therefore, you need to ensure that you earn your return on investment. However, you also need to attract your clients. This can only happen if you offer free samples. You should also consider focusing on promotional merchandise since it'd raise brand awareness while associating your brand with some element of generosity.

Hold Events to Spearhead Your Marketing Efforts

Perhaps you have heard that many consumers are more into the experience offered by the seller than the product. That is partly true. In many cases, the knowledge garnered from a marketing firm will determine the number of return clients.

Being a business professional, you need to incorporate brand awareness events to help consumers in learning more about your products. This is because they are an excellent brand awareness tool. However, as a small business owner, the concept of spearheading a brand awareness event may not hold some weight currently. Other than that, your brand awareness event must embody your brand's message.

Why Gamification Works Well In Enhancing Brand Experience

Gamification refers to the application of various game mechanisms to pre-existing non-gaming contexts. In the digital marketing world, business professionals use gamification in creating fun as well as engaging content. A significant number of them are focused on implementing gamification in their business. In the next five years, gamification strategies will be the standard practice for enhancing brand engagement. Besides, gamification will foster consumer loyalty. Here are some tips to assist you in realizing the benefits of gamification in revolutionizing content marketing.

- *Take small steps.* Conduct a pilot test based on the rate your product is likely to be consumed to learn how the theory works. You may begin by rewarding users who visit your site.

- *It is essential to relate gamification with your marketing goals.* You should ensure that the strategy you select helps you in creating product awareness. By using this brand awareness strategy, you will also be in a position to increase your firm's bottom line. The game needs to direct your guests to various parts of the firm's website for them to learn more about the products offered.

Hold a Social Media Consumer Contest

A social media contest is one of the leading ways through which a seller can engage with the target audience. It is also known as a strategy that can be utilized in creating brand awareness while building the local community around a specified brand. There are different tips you can use in ensuring that you conduct a unique social media contest. For starters, you can run a successful social media contest based on a specific type of theme. In this case, the theme should please the demands of your customers.

Engagement

In business, customer engagement refers to the connection between external shareholders and organizations using different channels of communication applied to seek correspondence. The connection may be a priceless reaction or interaction that affects the overall customer experience. Since connecting online is all about sharing, space allows you to successfully engage your clients using minor effort to build rich excellent customer experiences.

To be successful in creating a rich customer engagement platform, you may:

- Publish social campaigns
- Hold direct conversations with clients on your website
- Engage in relevant discussions based on your social networks

We live in a digital world. Making money has never been this easy. This is appended to the fact that people can now gain access to the internet. One decade ago, it was rare for various business professionals to gain access to online platforms. Any time they managed to do so, it would be on their laptops. Currently, many people own a mobile phone, giving them a direct connection to the internet. With access to the internet, are you making the most of it in your business? With the digital era taking over the world, you need to equip yourself with tips on how to make it.

Chapter 9: Tracking Your Marketing Efforts with Google Analytics

Google Analytics is a free service by Google that informs you on how users are interacting with your site. It uses a tracking system that you install on different pages of your website. Through a unique tracking code, you can sort your visitors through various dimensions. Using a JavaScript code, the system tracks user activity on the site and sets a cookie on the visitor's computer to create user IDs.

Importance of using Google analytics

Audience Analysis

Through Google analytics, you can see how many users are visiting your site and if they are new or returning. You can also get further details on their age, gender and how much time they spend on your site. This information helps you know what kind of audience you attract and whether your campaigns are effective or not.

Measure the Effectiveness of Content

Creating content for blogs is very expensive and time-consuming for it not to yield results. With Google analytics, content creators can know how many people read each blog article. This helps to understand what the bounce rate is and which articles perform better than others do.

Track Social Media Presence

Social media helps you connect with your customers and increases brand awareness. Tracking your different social media platforms will help you know where you receive the most traffic. This will determine where to invest more time in and allocate more budget for improvement.

Track on Site User Behavior

This provides details on which users visit your site, which outlet leads them to your site, and what they do once they are on your page. It informs the marketer on whether people are converting or not and at which point. It shows the most visited pages and the number of people that drop off at particular pages. This informs the marketer's decision on how to improve and make people stay longer on the site and make purchases

How to Set Up and Use Google Analytics

To begin collecting website data, you need to sign up for an account with Google Analytics. Visit the official analytics page, select "sign up" or "start for free". After this, a page describes the three steps to getting started and a sign-up button.

- Signing up and leaving a few details about the website you'd like to monitor
- Google will provide a tracking code that you will paste in the backend of your website pages
- Get analysis on your website pages in just a few hours

Set Up Conversion Goals

Having a lot of traffic on your digital platforms does not necessarily mean having many sales. With Google Analytics, you'll be able to tell your conversion rate when visitors click on pages like the newsletter or download page, contacts page, eCommerce page and such. Goals are set up to track conversions e.g. online sales and phone call requests.

How Google Analytics Works

It involves the use of a tracking code to track your visitors once they visit your site. Once a user reaches your page, Google analytics drops a cookie to collect information on user behavior and presents findings in different results. On your Google analytics homepage, there is a brief overview of how your website is performing. The information available includes active users, sessions, bounce rate, and session duration. There are five reporting options on Google analytics namely Real-time, acquisition, audience, Behavior, and conversion.

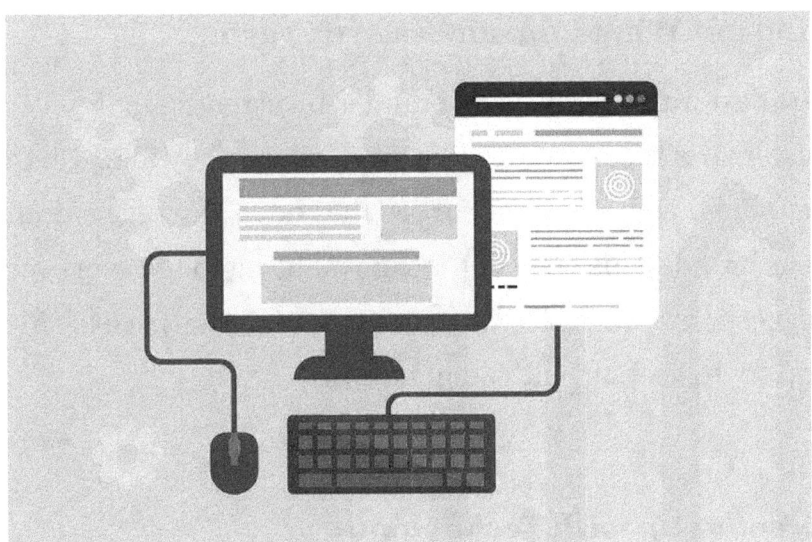

Chapter 10: Growing Your Brand

You do not need to be making loses with your business for you to decide on a rebrand or brand improvement. Growing as a brand requires constant improvement strategies. These may be in your marketing methods or changes to your products and services. Either way, do not remain monotonous; consumers easily forget a brand, hopping onto whatever is *hot* in the industry.

Find out What Consumers Are Craving

The best way to grow your brand is by listening to the customers. What do they like? What don't they like? Do they have any needs unattended? Do they have any suggestions for your brand? This does not mean you bring to life every nitty suggestion brought to you by a customer. Analyze each idea and try to keep up with competitors.

Keeping Up with Technology

What is new in the technology world, and how can you incorporate it into your brand? One thing is for sure; every day there is a new update on technology. Find those that fit in your industry and try to apply them to your business. Keep consumers excited and anticipating the next release.

Go Back to Your Strategic Plan

In the initial stages, an entrepreneur is also advised to create a 2 to 5-years strategic plan. This plan contains ideas on how the owner would like to grow the business over time. Most people start to make some good profit and forget their goals and dreams. Dust off that plan and peruse to see what you can apply to improve your brand.

Incorporate More Things as You Go

Do not just sell one thing until earth drops. Switch up or add new items. If you are selling vanilla ice cream, incorporate new flavors as you go. One or two flavors at a time to keep people interested. If you are selling mobile phones, include phone accessories like phone rings, phone covers, screens, and such.

Occasionally, run a clearance sale and give amazing offers. Surprise your customers with a fun competition. Do something other than the norm to keep your brand's name in customers' minds.

Brand Growth Beginner Challenge

Exercise;

- ✓ Write down 3 major things you would like to incorporate in your business as it grows (this is more like a strategic plan).
- ✓ Also, write down where you'd like to see your business in 2025, in terms of:
    - Size of company.
    - Social media following.
    - Number of employees.
    - Annual profit margin, etc.

Chapter 11: Advantages of Social Media Marketing for Business

Marketing businesses are indeed becoming profitable for the majority of individuals who are capable of managing them. MLM companies are becoming popular with individuals who are looking for ways to make money very easily through several methods. MLM businesses shall be paid for the individual sales they manage to make. Distributors can also create a downline, a network of individuals that the distributor has recruited to the MLM sector, and receive revenue from the sales of their downline. This only means that the more broad and broader the downline, the more the dealer can earn. To order to achieve such a downline company made up of many individuals and to sell your products to customers, you should have a vast network of personal contacts already in place. Nevertheless, not all individuals who wish to take part in the MLM business are very well acquainted with a lot of people, and this is becoming quite a challenge.

Multi-level marketing distributors are looking for ways to produce leads to push through sales and to have a more prominent downline organization. Traditional marketing strategies are most commonly used by new entrants to the

MLM business sector and by those who so readily stick to tradition and ignore inventions and technologies that have already been proven to be more successful. These approaches often use flags, posters, and flyers that may prove to be costly. Apart from being a little pricey, these promotional materials have now become useless and meaningless, because most people today prefer not to take notice of them. Their busy schedule usually prevents them from spending a few minutes on such things. We are now moving to the Internet and depending on it for these marketing materials.

Marketers must keep pace with changing times to meet the needs of the community effectively. This generation experienced the beginning of another age. Technology has fundamentally changed the world we once knew and changed the way we perform those daily tasks. Technology enables us to save time, energy, and finance with breakthroughs and innovations. Simple activities are much easier to accomplish, and what was once difficult has now become practical. The Internet is one of the most critical developments that technology has brought to humanity. Through the Internet, we have access to a wide range of knowledge networks that can be found online. The Internet has also been influential in building bridges that span the differences between time and location. Communicating with each other has become much more comfortable. Through social networking sites and similar networks, contact between regions and time zones apart has become simpler and much more affordable. To the astute MLM businessman like yourself, this can very well mean an abundance of possibilities for the lead generation. Using the Web as a tool to improve your MLM company can very well decide your future as an entrepreneur.

The Internet is something you and any MLM business owner can look into. It has become an essential medium for communications, though often challenged as a poor substitute for face-to-face contact and relationships. People find it much easier to communicate with each other and people with whom they share interests. More so, regular and consistent communication with each other can genuinely prove to be an excellent substitute for the personal touch that people look for when they engage in relationships with others. It also reduces the high expense of traditional advertising materials. You can also save time and energy, both of which can be spent on other activities that will help to further your MLM business. What's more, there are also several options on how you can develop your MLM business online.

Social media marketing is one of the most popular and effective Internet marketing techniques. Their success can be attributed to the fact that social media have become part of popular culture. Facebook, in particular, is one of the most social media sites that allows people from across the country or the globe to interact with each other regardless of the difference in time zones. People are able to make more friends through social media than they could have imagined. Social media marketing usually involves social networks and other aspects of online advertising. Social media sites often provide marketers with knowledge about consumers ' likes and dislikes. For example, Facebook shows ads in the profiles of its users concerning their likes and preferences, as indicated on their personal information. This makes it possible for advertisers to reach the targeted traffic and nothing more. It helps you to get the best value for whatever you pay for your social networking site. More than that, you will reap a lot of benefits from social media marketing.

The advantage of social media marketing is that it's a generally fun and enjoyable strategy to use. You will connect with people you may not have been able to meet without social media. You get to know these people, and ultimately you create a relationship that goes beyond the company but includes intimacy and friendship. You do a lot of good with your MLM company while also bringing fun to your life through social media marketing.

As described above, social media marketing is a cost-effective method that you can use to grow and develop your MLM business. Using it will not require a lot of money from you, as it is often charged for every button, if not for free. Posts and reviews from satisfied customers and downline members greatly enhance your reputation and help your company. This is open and is usually driven by word of mouth. PPC ads on social media platforms only hit targeted users, as Facebook and other websites only post advertising for your company on the profiles of those who are genuinely interested in it, as stated in their details and viewed from their likes.

Social media marketing is also successful in attracting traffic to your website or blog, potentially leading generation. Users also trust whatever information is shared on the social networking site or the social media platform because they see it as a reliable source. As a result, they won't hesitate to visit your blog or website and trust you and your company a little more because you're backed up by the social media platform.

One crucial advantage of social media marketing is that you can provide much-needed customer service and support. You have constant communication with the current clientele and can answer the question of investigative leads. You can do this without spending a lot of money, not to mention time and energy.

Furthermore, social media networking offers the same advantages that conventional offline marketing has to bring. More than that, it scales all the benefits to a whole new level. Transactions and messages are quicker, simpler, and more accessible!

Social media marketing has a lot of advantages. These are just a few, and you should devise a marketing strategy for social media that will ensure success for your multi-level marketing company.

Social Media Marketing Guide for Beginners

Social Media Marketing is a method of increasing awareness and web traffic across social media sites. In this process, typically innovative content to reach the masses through ads coming from a third-party source of confidence needs to be created throughout order for people to share the content of their interest with others and to build a vicious chain that would make business cover and go beyond the intended target audience. Each online marketer needs a goal, a product, a service, and a cause to promote through the vast and overwhelming World Wide Web. If you already have these things established in your mind, then congratulations! That could be the toughest part of getting into the social media challenge, and from now on, any attempt will help to achieve those goals effectively and flawlessly before you put your foot on the rank of the Social Media Guru.

The world of social media is broader and broader than ever before. It is a very strategic marketing platform that targets different cultures, ages, beliefs, genders, places, desires, and so on, making it the perfect medium to attract and target the right audience and achieve total success. The whole world doesn't care about video games, for example, but only the people who play video games are part of their interests. When you target a male audience with high heel advertisements on sale, some of them might go and buy a pair or two for their wives, but a couple or two isn't exactly the kind of effect you want to have. Therefore, you focus on specific age groups and certain other factors that cause some services and products, videos, and news to go "viral."

First, you need to know the primary social media sites.

Facebook

Holding more than 900 million users if you're already a Facebook user; this might not be new to you. Still, there are a lot of features worth mentioning. You can create a dedicated business page and interact directly and free of charge with your customers by posting free images, items, and videos of the service you want to provide or of the product you are trying to sell. This way, you can build a database of people who share your posts with their friends and thus create a never-ending chain. Most of these social media sites provide seamlessly mobile integration so that users, whether they're a portable Computer, a laptop, a tablet, or a mobile phone, are always connected to the internet in a way that you should take advantage of. People log in to Facebook, in any case, when moving, in the park, at home, at school, at work. Then you're there, selling your company to be shown in the news feeds, and you'd be there, continually playing the mind trick game to the point where people will find something exciting and worth searching out for their interests. Some big corporations like Starbucks, Microsoft, Samsung, Rockstar, Pepsi, etc. are doing the same thing, and it works perfectly!

Blogs

Blogs are a convenient way for people to connect in a semi-professional way when it comes to content quality. Quality content is always the key to good writing and, thus, to proper blogging. There are several content management CMS blogs where you can get yours up and running for free in less than 5 minutes, some of them Blogger, WordPress, and perhaps the most user-friendly one, Tumblr. One of the tricks here is to know your audience, your business, who you are approaching, and what you want to do with it. Now, this has to do with any SEO or Search Engine Optimization awareness, that is, using the right keywords to rank as high as possible in the search engine, i.e., Google, Bing, guy. It has to be linked to your posts, and, at the same time, you have to make sure that you use a keyword search tool to test the competition and the number of searches this keyword has. The lower the game and the higher the number of searches it receives in a month, the more convenient it is for you. If you were to advertise your website offering a technical support chat service, you would have to make the keywords very descriptive so that people looking for your service can notice you first. It's, for example, technical support for Windows, and then you're going to have to include specific words as if you were going a little straighter to the point. Since the competition would be reliable and Windows technical support is a wide range of content, you would concentrate and go further with the specific services that your company provides, adding additional keywords to go straight to the point would be the most successful way to do so. You would rank higher in the search engine, and people would find your product easily. From "Technical Support Chat" to "Technical Support Chat for Windows 7 and XP," you can see how the scope of the service you provide has narrowed, making it more precise, more comprehensive and more competitive with support for mobile operating systems, cell phones, Mac, iPhone, Windows Vista, Windows 8 and so on, and those places that offer services you are not connected to will not steal your ch Once you have understood the keyword concept, you can proceed and create content on a blog that would be easy to find by including the right tags on the search engine.

Then you'll have social media incorporation in the blog area again. There are many ways to share the content of your blog. Most Content Manager Services, like Tumblr, have social media buttons to post and like or don't like. You need to look for options to allow them (in rare cases, they are not enabled by default), so each of your posts would have shared buttons on Tweeter, Google+, Twitter, etc. and a blog on your associated blogging network. Through excellent quality and eye-catching content, you inspire people to share your stories on other media sites, such as those listed above, plus sharing them, and there, you have high chances to reach a wider audience.

Twitter

A fast-growing, popular social media platform. With more than 340,000,000 tweets a day and about 140,000,000 users worldwide, this site appeals to businesses and corporations as well as celebrities, artists, actors, everybody! A tweet is a message with a limit of 140 characters that you can write and upload, which followers can read and see at any time in their news feeds. Speaking about it, engaging directly, and starting new discussions is one of the things that makes this platform incredibly successful. We watch Kim Kardashian and read and think about everything she tweets in a day, the same as we can do with advertising and marketing campaigns for brands and products of their interest.

One hundred forty million users reaching the right audience may seem like a difficult task, but seeing it from the other side of the coin means more potential business customers. Once you get into the already described vicious chain of any social media site, things just keep coming on their own, and the first thing you'll notice is that hundreds of people are interested in your brand, thinking about it, reviewing it, and telling others about events, broadcasting, and so on.

Linkedin

Maybe a not-so-popular platform that makes it annoying for some people, but a very competent and strategic one for the rest. Most people won't spend long hours texting or talking to others about annoying, trivial things; instead, this social network is going straight to the point. People on Facebook and Twitter, for example, follow anyone's interest in merely socializing as well as businesses and corporations. Still, Linkedin's goal is to filter and leave the fun behind to concentrate more intensely on social media expertise.

On Linkedin, you can be part of a person searching for a job/service or part of a company offering a job/service. You can either create a personal profile with your professional information about yourself, research, contact information, interests, certifications, identifications, etc. or create a business or company page just as you do on Facebook or Twitter for the same purpose: share information about your brand, service, product and keep your fans and followers up to date with the latest updates.

YouTube

YouTube is a trendy forum. People are going to watch videos of any kind or be guided to any website that has a backlink to it or search engines. Once the people are there, you have a couple more "Featured Examples" on the column on the right side of the screen. Clicking from video to video will make you discover things you never thought you would find, exciting trends, funny videos, how-to videos, advertising, etc. Your chances of being seen are incredible, and you can also get people to subscribe to your channel, which is, in other words, your own YouTube room where you post your videos. Some people find it more exciting and more comfortable to watch a video than to read a whole post. You've got the graphics tool. If you're promoting fashion clothes, and that's the aim of all of your social media marketing, you can, along with other choices, upload a video of people modeling your clothes, redirect people to your primary business site, recommend people to share your video, sign up for future video updates, visit your fashion blog, like your Facebook page, follow you on Tweeter, Google+, Lin Close your eyes and try to imagine the Tree Diagram of the entire Social Media Marketing Strategy and how it can potentially reach any corner of the World Wide Web. Ambitious, isn't that?

Google+

A relative newcomer to the social media site battle, Google+ offers the integration of a variety of services, including Gmail, Google+ Basics, Google+ Circles, that allow you to share information or "profile" in a way that Facebook does, but has less popularity so far. You've got a "Flow" feature close to Facebook's News Feed that would let you see what the others are doing.

The company is very appealing to professionals and business networks because of the exclusivity and convergence of resources. For example, you build a Gmail account and, unless you disable it, by default you have access to all of these services and a profile that is ready to be updated with an image, contact information, etc. You have access to the entire Google+ network, including Gmail, YouTube, You+, Circles, Basics and even the well-known search engine that saves and shows results to the most relevant things for you. It is useful to have a spare Google+ account for any Social Media Marketer because of its potential versatility and because no source is too small or too much in marketing. It might not have the same effect, a 30 second commercial on TV as a tiny billboard on a bus, but the more you get the message, the better the results you get.

Social Media Statistics

According to the latest 87 research carried out on social media marketing up to 2012, this strategy from businesses to consumers named B2C or Business to the Community has risen to 16 per cent of customer engagement but is likely to grow to 57 per cent over the next 5 years. More than 30% of the world's population is now permanently online or has some kind of access to the web. More than 1/5 of the consumer's free time is spent on social media sites, hitting nearly 250 million tweets and 800 million Facebook updates on a daily basis. In the United States alone, more than 80 per cent of active online users spend their time on social media sites or forums. 60 per cent of people use 3 or more digital methods of product comparison analysis, prices and information on their planned purchases, 40 per cent use social media sites such as Twitter, or simply redirected from one of these sites, contributing to even direct interactions with retailers regarding posted offers.

Approximately 56 percent of Americans have one to three accounts on a social media site, 55% of whom are between 45-55 years of age and at least one profile.

Search Engine Optimization (SEO) details

70 percent of the links search users click on are organic. 46% of all searches are for product or service information. Half of all local searches are made on mobile devices. 66% of new customers use search and online research to find local businesses. There are 863 million websites worldwide that reference "SEO." There are 9.1 million searches performed each month, including acronyms, with the top two keywords being "SEO services" and "SEO business." More than 60,000 Twitter users have "SEO" in their profiles, 13 million blog posts have been written, including "SEO" in the title, and Amazon.com has almost 2,700 different SEO books. 93 percent of online experience begins with a search engine. B2B businesses that manage active content such as blogging and SEO services have increased their total website traffic by an average of 25 per cent over the past year, while those who have ignored SEO have seen an average 15 per cent decrease in overall visits. 21 percent of all time spent online is spent on web-based searches. The three main search engines Google, Bing and Yahoo! are among the five most-visited sites on the

Internet. Given that AOL is #7 and Ask is #10, five of the top 10 places most visited on the internet are search engines.

In addition, Social Media Marketing is an area where advertising experts and amateurs can come across their own ideas and plans to incorporate their own techniques. There is no Social Media Marketer university or college degree, this knowledge, which should be acquired through extensive research, needs to be constantly employed and tested in the desired field. It's a new approach that has torn down the old TV advertisement tactics that have moved it to the online market. The percentage of people who choose to go online on a computer or a capable tablet as opposed to people watching TV is growing steadily every single day. Statistics show that Social Media Marketing has a lower percentage of impact compared to the legacy of advertising, but the potential it has and room for growth is undoubtedly overwhelming and could be much better and more interactive than TV has been in the past decades.

The Impact of Social Media Marketing on Tourism

Lebanon is ranked 170th in the world (CIA, 2014). It is smaller than Connecticut, one of the smallest states in America. Lebanon is also one of the few democratic countries in the Middle East world. Concerning its currency, Lebanon is a free market economy and has a long tradition of laissez-faire economics. In addition to its coastal location on the eastern Mediterranean coast, Lebanon is considered to be the central' window' of the Middle East to Europe, North Africa, and the rest of the world. Because of this, the economy has gone through some very prosperous times, and it was once dubbed the Middle East ' Paris' before the nation's 15-year bloody civil war ended in 1990.

Moreover, although Lebanon is a small country, it is also one of the most diverse nations in the world. Christians, Muslims, Druze, and other minority groups are distributed throughout the small government, and even Lebanon's political system is based on sectary power-sharing.

Nevertheless, this diversity played a pivotal role in the problems of the country. This diversity was a necessary condition of the country's sectary civil war and still plays an essential role in its political stagnation. However, other factors (mainly foreign ones) are also to blame. There is currently no acting President, and rival political parties in the country continue to fight and prevent rather than facilitate the development of the country.

Lebanon's proximity to Israel has also made it a foreign policy/proximity battleground for foreign nations, each using Lebanon for its selfish ends.

The tragic political realities of the country have caused significant damage to the economy of the country. Moreover, since Lebanon is a service-based economy, this particular sector has had the most significant impact.

Tourism plays a vital role in the nation's economy "Tourism has long been one of Lebanon's leading economic fields" (Economic Research Unit, 2010).

The World Travel & Tourism Council also reported that the travel & tourism industry in Lebanon contributed more than $4 billion in 2013 (World Travel & Tourism Council, 2014).

The travel & tourism industry accounted for about 10% of the economy in 2012, but this share fell to 9% in 2013 (ibid., p. 14). This is due, as well as some other factors, to the political situation in the country. Also, the number of tourist arrivals in the country declined from 2011 to 2013.

Since the tourism industry has been somewhat blurred in the last few years, the room for error has become very limited for companies in this market. Political & economic conditions are stressing tourism-related (TR) businesses in Lebanon. This means that these companies are forced to do more to make up for increasing losses (or declining profits) with fewer resources. It is not clear when the political and economic situation in Lebanon will improve, especially since the civil war in neighboring Syria shows no signs of decline.

There are many ways in which Lebanese TR companies can adjust during these periods, such as by introducing downsizing policies and slashing marketing and advertising budgets. As economic recessions and hard times hit companies, marketing budgets are usually the first ones to be reduced. But mainly because TR companies need to do more marketing to make up for lost businesses, this may not be a good idea.

One solution to this problem is to take advantage of social media marketing tactics because they cost little or no money, which is ideal for the current economic situation in Lebanon. Social media marketing helps TR companies to conquer the barriers of limited budgets and reduced revenue.

Problem Statement

Over the last few years, the positive impact of social media on the industry has been extremely high (Kaplan et al., 2010; Stelzner, 2010; Treem & Leonardi, 2012, p. 143; Baker & Green, 2014).

Facebook and Twitter fans of a specific brand are much more likely to recommend and buy from these brands than non-fans (Cruz & Mendelsohn, 2011). But you don't need to make sure that social media has an impact on business through research. This is attributed to social media users, who account for more than 30% of the population. More and more companies are putting social media marketing tools into their marketing strategies, and, in some cases, they have become an essential part of their overall business strategy.

Of course, one would expect Lebanon's businesses to quickly take Social Media Marketing as a critical role in their overall marketing strategies, but that is not the case. Concerning the Middle East, and in particular Lebanon, the world is far behind the West in the use of social media. Not only that, there is a lot of room for growth when it comes to businesses involved in the tourism industry. No spending on technology holds tourism companies away from exploiting social media marketing opportunities.

The Lebanese tourism industry is not taking advantage of the marketing tactics of social media, even though the benefits of doing so are clear. This is a significant problem, particularly since the economy is going through a tough time.

However, Lebanese TR companies and businesses in Lebanon usually do not follow social media resources as they should. This presents a massive waste of resources issue as well as substantial missed opportunities as a broader target audience can be reached via social media, allowing companies that embrace social media marketing platforms to achieve a better chance of success and prosperity.

Purpose of the study

However, as long as no research is undertaken on the successful implementation of a social media marketing strategy in Lebanon, many TR companies may be lost even if they decide to adopt social media marketing tools.

Also, while numerous studies have been performed in the West on the successful application of social media marketing strategies, the findings of these studies may or may not extend to the Lebanese context. It is, therefore, also the purpose of this study to identify specific factors related to the successful implementation of social media marketing among Lebanese TR companies.

There is no question that social media marketing plays a vital role in marketing campaigns and even in the overall success of tourism-related businesses.

Lebanon Tourist-Related (TR) companies are far behind the developed world in spending and using SMM. Since there are many advantages to SMM, why is that so? Also, to catch up with the rest of the planet, what is the most effective way for Lebanese TR companies to implement the SMM campaign? The goal of the study was, therefore, to find the reasons for such investment and use of SMM by Lebanese TR companies and to guide these companies in the successful use of SMM.

Methodology

The purpose of this analysis is twofold. The goal of this study is to find out precisely what are the factors that prevent the widespread adoption of social media marketing tools among Lebanese TR companies. The theory used is interpretivism, an inductive approach that goes from limited to extensive research, an ethnographic technique, and a methodological methodology. In-depth interviews with ten participants from ten different companies are used. Five businesses had high visibility in social media, and the other five did not. The participants' responses have, therefore, provided beneficial information and solutions to the research issue.

Findings

The results found that among the most relevant factors for the limited expenditure and use of SMM by Lebanese TR firms, many do not see the advantages of using SMM and therefore do not endorse it.

The findings also provided useful information on reasons for the successful adoption of SMM by Lebanese TR firms, including the acceptance of SMM by the owners / decision-makers and the value of these people in seeing the benefits of SMM. Also, problems with the implementation of SMM include negative feedback from customers and inter-departmental power struggles.

Recommendations include the clarification of the advantages of SMM to Lebanese TR businesses, which are of such great importance for them to use SMM. A precise schedule of days to add content to social media sites, as well as a thorough tracking of SM user comments on the company, should also be included in the SMM strategy.

The researcher hopes that the analysis would help shed light on the critical aspects of SMM and its relationship with Lebanese TR companies. It is also expected that the recommendations will be taken into account by the Lebanese TR firms.

How to Boost Your Business With Standardization of Responses

There are inadvertent cringes about terms like "standardization" these days. Correctly, this could be attributed to the need to cultivate individuals in companies and to the promotion of open-ended and creative thinking among employees. While this strategy has proven to be efficient in developing creativity and free-form approaches, it may not be as effective in roles that require more routine responses, such as support and operations.

The confusion around non-standardized responses could hurt an organization in a variety of ways.

1. Task confusion

If workers are unaware of their roles, find out that they have done redundant work, are humiliated by not understanding the previous meaning when talking to a customer, or discover that they have given wrong instructions-they have been the victims of task misunderstanding or uncertainty. Task misunderstanding arises when workers do not have (or know about) access to the right knowledge base, collection of procedures, or recognize their responsibilities.

Job misunderstanding has been related to a long-term decline in productivity and employee satisfaction. It is essential for reps whose primary work involves responding to stakeholders to provide clarity in their responses to internal and external stakeholders.

What to do about it: explain the goals and responsibilities of the reps in their position. To ensure that there are no overlaps, consider setting up a forum where everyone can submit new written responses to share their experience and managing strategies with the rest of the team. Not only will this lead to a more open culture, but it can also save the next person time, they need to find the right way to deal with the situation.

The naming and cataloging of responses are, therefore, also crucial; it is essential to implement policies that can be easily recognized and implemented. Do you remember a time when you needed to find something in a shared work folder and couldn't find-anything-because it seemed out of place?

Onboarding new reps well will also improve the transparency of responsibilities and ensure that there is a consistent and thorough framework in place for the future. Having this transparent repository will also help new reps find and use resources that will help them ramp up faster.

2. Response uncertainty

Almost every day, there are new questions that can be posed to the reps. Often, only very seasoned reps will know what needs to be asked and answered. Nonetheless, it could be extremely challenging for most reps to have a clear idea of precisely what to ask for so that they can begin to resolve issues.

On the other side of the table, consumers may want to respond accurately, but they do not have a structure for precisely what they need to provide to re-create or explain the problem. Also, if reps do not ask diagnostic questions in a standardized and easily manageable way, clients may not know precisely how to handle their issues.

Ambiguities in the answer can be a stumbling block for both sides, as lack of clarity contributes to a subsequent uncertainty in the search for a solution as well.

What to do about it: categorize the types of specific questions and answers needed to address 70-90 percent of all issues related to the product or its auxiliary services. In providing groups of recurring and essential themes, it's easier for the reps to identify the right information they need to collect to get going.

Putting questions in formats also helps clients to reduce their anxiety, because they feel that they are being served attentively and that they are asking relevant and concise questions about their issues. However, having a standard response (like a "shape" to fill) also helps to keep anxiety from a lack of expectations down-as long as it's not too long!

3. **Inconsistent customer experience**

It is sometimes convenient for us to presume that when workers come on board, they already have some pre-requisite knowledge of what they are supposed to do. But this, and some elements of miscommunication, also happen day-to-day, and that makes it difficult for reps to respond to customers consistently.

For consumers, we've probably experienced circumstances when service reps gave us conflicting orders. Not only do they not necessarily solve issues, but they can also make it extremely difficult for customers.

Sometimes the level of service also varies depending on the context of the person answering. For example, with the emergence of dispersed teams, more reps are working away from their office or on their mobiles or tablets. This means that sometimes it's hard for them to navigate any saved files without jumping through hoops to get to a secret folder somewhere-and when they get there, they have to copy and paste on a small screen before sending it off.

As a high-interactivity touchpoint, customer service can build or ruin a customer relationship, and therefore businesses need to pay close attention to enhancing it as much as possible. Frustration can also often lead to discontent in the workplace.

What to do about it: consider having an easily accessible Knowledgebase of Responses, where employees can quickly refer to it and take it with them whenever they need it. Have someone regularly monitor and curate the responses that reps use, and make sure the tools are easily accessible to everyone who wants them, through networks and devices. If your team is scattered or mobile, it's even more critical to have a simple, mobile-centric solution where reps can easily select and submit answers.

Install best practices among service organizations-Understand the service chain through analysis, then do your best to identify bottlenecks and difficulties. Using examples with your reps in the middle of it, and discuss how to develop your internal resources or skills to help them do their job better.

4. Non-contextual understanding

Context is defined as physical, emotional, and environmental factors in the context of a situation. Of example, when someone talks about something, you need to go beyond what they say:* What they saw and experienced at the point in time* How they felt about it and what they were feeling* What kind of atmosphere were they in: a busy and noisy place or a peaceful office space? Contextual comprehension can help to sort problems much more quickly and lead to better solutions. For example, realizing that your customer is waiting for your product or service to operate on a crowded sidewalk in the slumbering sun is a complex concept that you need to take into account when managing the situation like a pro.

Such aspects are often not addressed when dealing with customers. When words are taken at face value, it makes it extremely difficult to understand what the problem is and how you can use your input from the consumer to develop the next version of the product or service. It's just giving up essential sources of product guidance and development.

Language barriers can also prove to be an obstacle for empathizing with customers. Several times, whether collaborating with partners or supporting customers, we know that not coping with cultural or linguistic issues can disrupt communication and expectations.

What to do about it: define the significant contextual factors that occur during and influence the use of your product. What is the typical situation that your product will be used for? Write a story about it and draw a story map that describes the process. First, consider edge cases where other small groups of consumers might instead use the commodity, and write their stories as well.

Exchange these ideas with your reps. Get input from them and refine the story, and help them understand the importance of discussing them in their response and language.

You can also create models of reactions that reps can use to easily identify such factors quickly, without taking too much effort at their end to memorize at the beginning-though it may become more straightforward and more intuitive later on. This will also help to bring new reps and fresh grads into the business.

If you have in-house language counsel, let them review some of these response models and translate them / add cultural nuances to them. Otherwise, some outside support in refining the language and strategy could prove beneficial in your dealings with customers as well.

5. Increased back and forth

One of the most subtle drawbacks of not getting consistent answers is the loss of time. If reps have responded previously in a certain way or sequence, there is typically a rationale to improve efficiency in such ways.

Occasionally, the reps are not sure what to say (see #2) and thus end up spending a much longer time solving a problem than would have been necessary. Leaving detailed questions or explanations almost always contributes to the need for more time to go back and forth with the correspondent to clarify what they are experiencing or what they need.

Getting more back-and-forth instances frustrates both the stakeholder and the delegate, and wastes a lot more time that could have been spent on other productive activities.

What to do about it: compile and save the responses suggested and used previously by the reps. Through getting this validated theory or approach embedded in the answer, you can get to the root cause of the problem more efficiently and offer better solutions.

Towards better customer experience

The standardization of responses requires a systematic understanding of customer needs, products, reps' knowledge, and the answers needed to ease the process as a whole. While this may take some time, in the beginning, to evaluate and execute steps and models, it can yield significant benefits in the long run as reps feel more motivated and more productive, and customers feel happier.

Boost Your Business Profits Even in Tough Times

With revenues declining and costs rising, it's easy to get upside down in the profit column. With credit markets just beginning to thaw, it may be challenging to get the cash needed to continue the operation. And tight-fit customers won't let you sell your way back to profitability. How can profits be improved without increasing sales? The easiest way is to reduce prices.

Have you ever noticed how some firms seem to succeed in economic downturns and blow past their competitors? You don't want to be one of them?

You can do that! There are secret gold mines in your day-to-day business operations that you have been unable to locate using common sense, gut feeling, and trial-and-error. Through ordering, billing, buying, payment, and delivery processes, your consumers can encounter an error rate of 6-12-18 percent—an error rate that devours your income.

You can't advertise or sell your way out in a recession, as consumers are tightening their pocket strings. You can't innovate your way out, because consumers want validated solutions, not new, untested ones.

Nevertheless, you should continuously enhance your mission-critical operations-the removal of errors, delays, and waste, resulting in immediate profits. Don't wait! And best of all, your processes are entirely within your control-you don't have to rely on anyone else to achieve your goals.

This ensures that you can fill your sales dips with money that has been diverted to your operations. You can always turn the workers' attention to solving organizational problems.

While most businesses are cutting the normal costs-travel, training, incentives, salaries, and headcount-some are using this recession as an opportunity to improve their operation so that they can survive this economic storm and future ones as well. We know what only a few people seem to know: one in three workers work at the "Fix-It" factory in the business.

Fix-It Factory

Each company has two factories:

- one that produces and delivers the product or service;
- and a secret "Fix-it" factory that cleans up all the errors and glitches that arise in the other factory.

How do you know if you have a "Fix-It" factory? Just pay attention to the amount of time you spend on training, firefighting, and crisis management. Do you always depend on heroics to save the day? Are you praising firefighting, but not fire prevention? Do you have hordes of workers who are testing the finished product or service? If so, the "Fix-It" Factory would cost $20-$40 off every $100 you spend.

If you're a $1 million corporation, that's $250,000–$400,000. If you are a $100 million company, that's $20-40 million. Just imagine what you can do to save a fraction of that money for your productivity!

Fix Your System, Not Your Service, or Your People When there is an issue with a product or service, someone always wants to blame. Most of the time, the blame falls on the person who created the problem, made a mistake, or made a mistake.

It's false! Blame the step-by-step method that caused a person to make a mistake, error, or defect. Instead of punishing an individual, ask him to figure out how to change the process to avoid a future mistake. This is called the error-proofing.

We all benefit from the error-proofing. Without a foot on the brake, you can't start a modern car. Mistake testimony! You can't plug the electrical cord with the prongs inverted. Mistake testimony! With a little focused thinking, there's a way to make a mistake-proof of any operation.

Focus for Full Profit

While most people think that mistakes are spread evenly across companies like butter on bread, the fact is that errors tend to cluster in a few critical steps of the process. All you have to do is:

•count the number of mistakes you have made.

- Categorize by process stage, position, or other groupings.

- Take the largest group of bugs then.

- Analyze the root cause of the mistake.

- Change the method to avoid the error.

Just four out of every 100 steps were responsible for more than 50 percent of the flaws, errors, and defects. Fixing these mistakes in the "Fix-It" Factory will cost 10 to 100 times more than doing the right thing the first time. Poof, there's your profit.

Most of the businesses already count their mistakes, but few do anything with them except for the flog workers at the annual review. Would you be one of the few who use these statistics to find ways to make error-proof procedures and transfer workers out of the "Fix-It" Factory to the benefit of customers?

With a slow economy, there will never be a better time to work on these problems than now. Therefore, when the economy turns around-as, it always does-you will not only have more money, but you will be able to offer better rates than your rivals and still make huge profits.

Top 10 Ways to Find a Fix-it Facility

1. Heroes regularly struggle to avoid the distribution of a lousy product or service. One organization prided itself on "doing the unthinkable every day."

2. Complaints from the client. There are 16 more that won't tell you for every customer who complains about your product. Each of these says eight other people why they don't like your product or service. Word of mouth is going to kill you!

3. Complaints from the manufacturer. Are your suppliers moaning about the unreasonable last-minute requests you make and how long it takes to get paid? Word of mouth is going to kill you!

4. Employee whining: "I can't do my job because that's the way they don't do their job!" Employees want to do a good job. What's stopping them, huh?

5. Blaming people for their poor quality. Ninety-nine percent of the problem lies with your systems and processes, not with your people. It depends on your business operations.

6. Knee's dick fixes that crash. Common sense and gut feeling stop working at a 3% error rate. That's when you need the "popular science" of these tips to get you to the next point.

7. Margins are low; costs are high, development is stagnant. Defects and delays eat away at the margins and inflate the prices.

8. Failures on the ground. How big is the warranty or repair department? How many people do you need to handle your customer service and technical support calls?

9. Too many quality control inspectors. You can't check the consistency of your product or service, but you can put it in.

10. Absenteeism, turnover. Employees tend to do a poor job with their clients. Employees get angry when the internal system prevents them from doing a good job. How do your processes discourage your workers from doing a good job?

Quick and Easy Ways to Boost Your Business Profits

Did you know that there are a lot of things you can do on your website, blog, sales letter, or product that can have a dramatic impact on the size of your Paypal account?

You see, there are a million and one items available on the Internet, and so is the Internet population! It's all about the numbers making money online. Because Internet marketers can have hundreds to thousands of visitors visiting their website every day, even the smallest changes can dramatically increase their profits.

Branding: You can't afford to be too polite when you're trying to market your goods on the Internet. Your product and website on the Web are like a small drop in a vast ocean. People's attention is divided among millions of websites on the Internet that scream for their consideration. If you want to improve your online sales, you MUST be a branded product!

You see, the online world is somewhat different from the real world. Many people might be afraid to blow their horns in public (or tell others how much money they're making online). Yet online, you can write (almost) whatever you want on your sales copy or your profile page. The most important thing you need to do is to stand out from the rest of the crowd!

If you've achieved sales success, make sure you' flash' your Paypal screenshots in front of others. Do whatever it takes to let others know what is so amazing about you. Let them think you're different from each other. If you do unusual things, chances are, people will notice and spread the word. One of the things you need to remember about branding is that you have to let others know what you specialize in. Take, for example, Internet marketing blogs. When you're searching the whole blogosphere, you'll find hundreds of blogs out there named Web marketing with or blog about making money online. There are too many blogs about making money online or internet marketing, so the best way to stand out from the rest is to focus on a particular niche. If you're in SEO and you're good at long-tail slots, let others know more about it than concentrate on generic SEO branding. It's better to get a sub-niche than a general niche.

Use your imagination to design your own innovative:

Graphics enhancements: Many people out there ignore the nature of their products. They will spend tons of money on their ghostwriters, their blogs, their auto responders, and even their staff. Still, the moment they ignore the presentation of their E-cover, they lose many valuable sales because their E-cover is not appealing enough for their E-book.

The truth will scare you-many of them will judge a book by its cover. Mini-site banners are equally important. Imagine, the first thing people see is the banner itself, other than the first headline of the sales copy or landing page.

Don't use just any banner: There are tons of PLR books out there that come with the sales letter PSD file. You can also combine photos to make the full package look even more attractive.

Sales Copy Tweaks: The essential aspect of the sales process is to get the prospect's attention in a selling copy. The headline is, therefore, the most crucial aspect of the entire sales edition.

After all, if the headline does not get readers to read the rest of the sales letter, it makes no sense to publish the sales letter in the first place! Often when people look through a promotional file, a lot of them don't read the sales letter line by line. Often when people look through a promotional record, a lot of them don't understand the sales letter line by line. Fast And Easy Ways To Increase Your Business Profits We also search through a sales copy and arrive at the end of a sales copy only to see how much it costs. One of the best ways to reach out to these' scanners' is to use graphics to say an image.

For example: if you're selling a membership platform that provides the best content for resellers, you can tell them: "Would you rather catch small fish with what you're doing now or buy this membership, and your company can carry nothing but big fish?" Maximizing Niche Market Profits: Here are some four ways to tweak your site, and you'll be able to make more money.

1. **Use only one format when choosing your AdSense layout:** the more consistent your design, the easier it is for people to click on your ads. Your goal is to try to' mask' the ads to look more like links on the web page. Sometimes they may not know what they're clicking on AdSense, but at least it brings more money.

2. **Choose a color that fits with the context of your niche site:** once again, this will also boost clicks on the advertising, and, as a result, your sales will also increase.

3. **Try to find the AdSense ads where it's easier for people to see:** don't position them in places where people won't navigate either because that stops them from clicking on them (or even seeing them for that matter).

4. **Go to the appropriate keywords in your ads:** Google doesn't care about your content; just scans the title, definition, and URL. One of the easiest ways to promote a company at a niche site is to use a' review' style. Take, for example, a film. When someone goes online to read the review, they tend to believe the author and keep their opinion in mind when they go to the movies. Remember, however, that the person reading the review is likely to consider what the writer is saying. They're not sitting around worrying if the film critic is getting the partner money to tell people to watch the movie. Most of the time, Web marketers, or even niche marketers, become too' soldier' when it comes to partner product recommendations. We don't realize that an easy,' unbiased' review can easily influence the mind of the buyer. If you were to think about a product as if you were discussing it from a' fair' point of view, you would be able to get more traffic to your affiliate programs. It would help if you built titles for your articles, such as-ABC

product review, or XYZ product review. After all, people would rather trust a neutral party than a salesman.

Never Stop Testing: In short, you should always remember that Internet marketing and niche marketing are all about numbers. You must never fail to get as much traffic as you can because no amount of tuning can boost your sales by a lot if you don't have any traffic to start with.

Ways To Boost Your Business With Teleseminars

Teleseminars are a perfect way to look, sell, stay in touch with current customers and partners, create your list, and more. Here are just a few of the ways you can use teleseminars to improve your company.

Introduce a new product or service: Product launches are one of the most common means of using teleseminars. This is a perfect way to explain everything about what the company can do and how it can benefit your customers. This is particularly useful for educational goods, as the teleseminar can be mainly high impact material, with only a little bit of sales. There's no way in an hour to say everything in a novel, or even an ebook, so you can give the audience as much as you can and still leave them wanting more.

If you are in the service industry and have a new service, you should send a teleseminar to promote it to your current and prospective customers. If you are a mortgage broker and a new First Time Buyer initiative is in place, use a teleseminar to illustrate it to all your prospects at once. You can even have a question and answer session if you're enthusiastic about it.

Re-launch a product or service: If you have a product or service that has not earned enough attention lately, re-launch it. Attach a bonus or two or limited time and do a teleseminar to highlight this month's special. One of the things you can do with a re-launch is to have a few happy customers as guest speakers. Since they have already had time to use what you have to sell, they will give your prospects some useful information from the consumer.

Teach your customers how to use your product or service: Most products and services are not entirely self-explanatory. Having a teleseminar to tell you all about the unique features or extra services you have helps them to get the most out of your product or service. Not only does this make for great customer relationships, but it's rare enough to get the clients to speak to their buddies about how awesome you are. During the teleseminar, you can even ask for referrals.

Establish yourself as an expert: Have someone ask you during the teleseminar about your product or service. It's a perfect way to establish yourself as an expert in your profession. Who's being interviewed? Stars, celebrities, Nobel laureates. That's to tell experts. People are going to listen to that.

Create Report: People buy from people they know, want, and trust. Tell your viewers a little bit about how you came to be a lion tamer, a coach, or an insurance agent. Don't just try to sell something to them. Let them know you from the comfort of their living room. Please give them a little something before you ask for something else.

Tell the embarrassing story of when you got your 4X4 stuck in the mud, and the Volkswagen Beetle pulled you out. Then when you tell us about the towing service you created called "Beetle's Towing," they'll laugh at you, and they'll wonder about you when they get stuck, too.

Informative Prospecting: If you are in the service industry, you can help people to understand your field of expertise. A real estate agent may hold a teleseminar on the purchase of investment property. You could talk about tax breaks, appreciation, and professional management, so you don't have to get up in the middle of the night to deal with the tenants. You can also talk about some of the ways that deals can go wrong if you don't have a licensed agent involved, such as buying a building without checking what other links might be held against the property. Please give as much information as you can, while showing why it's a good idea to have expert help at the same time.

With a product, you can do the same thing. Don't just tell you how great your product is, though. Tell us all about the problems your product has to deal with, and some possible solutions. Then let us know how your product provides the most solutions at a reasonable price.

Preview Calls: A preview call is a call that advertises a later, more significant event. It's usually free, but you might have a paid preview call as well. For this type of teleseminar, you want to give as much useful information as you can, if you're previewing a weekend event, you can't possibly carry everything you're going to cover in one hour. So, choose a few topics and offer some great information and then tell them about the upcoming event. Please don't make this an infomercial about how fantastic the game is going to be-show them how great it's going to be by giving them a great call.

Build a FAQ or a whole new product: One of my mentors said, "When you hear the same question three times, it's time to make an answer for it." And, while you're telling people all about your beautiful products and services, you should document them, too. Once your teleseminar is finished, you can have your recording transcribed, and now you've got a FAQ sheet that you can use as a bonus to anyone who buys from you. You should put the record on your website so that people can listen to it. Let them send you their email and name to get access to it, and now you've got a mailing list.

Mix and Match: Other teleseminars can use several of these concepts. You can launch a company, create a report, and have an interviewer ask you all the right questions to make you look good. You will find out what your clients want to know the most and tell them about it on a Customer Service call, then tape it and put it on your website. There are endless possibilities.

Chapter 12: Facebook Marketing Tips for Business

Many business executives recognize the value of Facebook marketing and have taken the first step in creating a Facebook Fan Page for their company. But after the page is created, many CEOs drop the ball. They don't take full advantage of everything Facebook has to offer for their business Posting on Other Business Pages Facebook Fan Pages has evolved into a place where Pages can post and update on other Pages. You can like and comment on other sites in the "View" mode. You can write to your friends ' profiles in Page mode. Wall posts are no longer in chronological order, and you don't have much influence over the posts on your Pages. The good news as a Facebook admin is that you can view your page in chronological order. Click the "Admin screen" to do this under the "wall." It helps you to arrange your page by presenting it in an order that is easy to understand and maintain.

As you are in page view mode, if the name of your fan page is not your real name, as is the case with most fan pages (they are the name of the business), it is essential to add an identity to your post. If you're posting on other fan pages, go ahead and sign off with a dash and your first name at the end of your comment. It helps you add a personal touch to your posts and increases your engagement level.

Talk about how you're going to get across. Are you on the websites of your rivals because of a self-serving agenda, or are you there to contribute? Here is a suggestion that you do most of your networking in a business sector that is not the same as your (non-competitive) business. You can post on business pages that are related to yours, but not to your competitors. Maybe you'll get more results that way.

Prevent Spam on your Site Most business owners have found that, at times, their rivals would spam their sites. Facebook now has the spam plugins you can use to curve it. To access and use Facebook spam filters, this tool can be found under the "edit tab" and allows you to load keywords that are placed into the spam filter so that you, as an admin, can automatically delete messages. This is in "Admin View." Comments appear in a light color that some people have said is more difficult to see, but this method is still beneficial.

Notifications can be made by email, or you can turn it off by clicking the "edit tab." This is great because you can get updates when you get new fans or feedback.

Advertising tips :

1. *The Photo Strip is at the top of your tab.*

The pictures at the top of your page are the five most recently uploaded ones. You can delete them by clicking on the X in the right corner of each page.

The "Photo Strip" at the top works like a photo screen and the images pop up so that the viewer does not lose his place when he looks at the pictures. Have some custom graphics for the top 5 images on your list. They could be 970x 680 pixels. Here's a suggestion to leave white space around the edges of the pictures. FB is going to reduce them to a 97x 68 thumbnail. Using call-to-action images such as "click here," "find more," "for info," or "free download." The image will pop up when visitors click on that link. Place information and a call-to-action connection or phone number in the picture description so that visitors can quickly contact you.

2. *Links to the left side of your page.*

Reset the order of your ties on the left side of your Facebook page. If you have more than seven links, you will see a "more" link, and you can drag and drop those links from there. Place the "landing tab" at the bottom that is usually the "welcome" where visitors land. This way, when you visit your welcome page, all your links will be extended automatically, and you can see the full list of all your links on the left side of your page.

3. Make the most of Facebook iFrames by adding exciting content.

Facebook uses iFrames, and even though it's a bit more complicated, it allows you the ability to add photos, videos, and opt-in boxes and a call to action. You can have a whole page set up on your site and then add it to your iFrame on your Facebook page and make it your custom landing tab. Also, you can take Facebook ads and drag them to the landing pages and links on your Facebook page. It gives you the ability to test various deals and offerings. You can check and break your different offers on different iFrames links on your website.

4. Updates functionality provides the opportunity for free advertising on valuable Facebook real estate.

Click the "edit tab" "marketing" button. You can send updates to all your fans. All of these messages go to "all." You'll see an area called "Unread News" in the top right corner of Facebook. This is valuable real estate, and if you use "updates" more often than not, you can get your followers more interested in your fan page. If you have a viral post on your blog, you can take the exact link and add it to the "updates" so that your fans can see it on the top right corner of their screen. You will have free ads for yourself by using "updates," and it will appear at the top right-hand corner of your fans' pages.

5. Improve awareness and interaction with Facebook News Feeds.

Studies show up to 90% of your fans don't go back to your website after clicking the "like" button. Not to worry, however, because by maximizing your visibility in Facebook News Feed, you can still be visible to your fans and engage them to "remind" them about your business and increase visitors to your main website, which is the next step in improving your bottom line.

Tips to improve coverage on your fans' news page include:

- Post before noon in your time zone.
- Post one to two times a day.
- Don't over the message. Several businesses are importing tweets and "over-post." This can damage your "edge rating" (the metric that Facebook uses), which can ultimately lead to your posts appearing less and less in the news feed of your fans.
- Use your questions.
- Keep your posts short and simple.
- Be very intimate.

- Use the material of other users. Include photographs, videos, and ties. Create your strategies to make news feeds more visible.

By using these ideas, you can make Facebook more accessible and attract more fans.

Facebook Marketing Ideas and Tools

Each part of business and money-making seems to be upgraded now and then in today's fast-paced life. Today, the Internet is one of the most widely used mediums of communication as well as business. It is therefore not surprising that this platform has produced and built newer and more efficient ways of doing business, either by developing new or by extracting from existing segments, ideas, and resources that would support the business entity by using this vast method. One of the main aims of the Internet is to make work both easy and rewarding. More often than not, people operating on the net have contributed to this objective and have provided the general public, small production groups, and large companies with ways and means to market their services and products that are both burden-free and cost-effective. The social networking sites are one such avenue on the Internet, and the most prominent of them is' Facebook.'

Not only does it have one of the largest member populations in the world, but it also has probably the highest number of non-individual profiles or group/company profiles. So it's not shocking that we've seen a lot of marketing-based behavior and that, too, with success. But the most effective ones are based on picked, tried, and tested models, some of which will be shared with you in this chapter.

You need to build a Facebook profile page to start. It should be noted that this profile would be the face with which people around the globe would know you. Therefore, while creating a profile, care should be taken, and some source of attraction should be given to attract visitors and make them read it.

Being a networking site, Facebook naturally works to create a network that contains as many users and accounts as possible. It is, therefore, necessary for your profile to widen its reach. There are different ways to do this, such as building a linking chain, as well as groupings and groups.

Groups and communities are a significant marketing center and can be used for great results. You may set up a group of your own or participate in an existing society to show your products and services and then have feedback and discussions on them. It's contributing to costly advertising.

Updates to the status of your profile may also be of great use in this regard. As most people follow each other through status updates, it could be used to send more insightful messages about your products or services. Links and video files could also be uploaded to provide the specifications via status updates.

Using engaging titles and explanations on your profile page might turn out to be a difference between people who ignore or click your message. It is, therefore, obviously advisable to adorn your profile with enticing titles and even more captivating descriptions to get even the attention of a casual surfer.

A few years ago, Facebook came up with the idea of pages in response to the demands of marketing users. Such pages are an excellent medium for companies, particularly small and medium-sized ones, to make their presence felt on the social network. Also, several other features such as flash and other Facebook software other than HTML can be added to the list. So it can be personalized and used to the fullest.

Paying attention to the customer feedback and reviewing it now and then would go a long way towards developing your brand of products or services. Small details such as whether or not there is a rise in user traffic or what comments and feedback your profiles share will help you improve your performance and, in turn, leave an indelible impact on your brand.

One thing that needs to be taken care of if you want to get the most out of Facebook is that you don't have to sell in the face to be a good marketing strategist. The idea of "90/10" fits in with the Facebook public in terms of the rejection of what is offered. How often have you declined any sales strategy yourself? It means that Facebook is a social network, and therefore what will click here is that if one could offer a solution to the problems of others, then marketing would be achieved as they connect with others.

Another fundamental method is that one should give particular importance to filling in account settings and information. Mostly, it's a tendency among people to scuttle through different forms and jump up to get in contact with other specific users of interest or their mates. It should be noted, however, that the details of your profile will go a long way towards establishing a link between you and the visitor; therefore, it should be not only complete but also explanatory. Ample importance must, therefore, be given to this activity.

Very often, people who are out of habit or fear of competition do not reveal their ideas for the social benefit on such sites. On the contrary, this particular step will serve you well. Even if you share your thoughts on a forum or in a group that includes people with your kind of business interests, it's going to be very useful, as you might come across as an expert on the subject or as an authority.

You are adding a link to your Facebook account on other sites that you may have, or even blogs will do wonders to promote your profile and, in effect, your company. Most readers will undoubtedly have a Facebook profile, and it would be fascinating for them to visit the profile of the person who owns the site or blog they are reading, perhaps out of curiosity. Without a doubt, this would increase traffic and, in effect, a word of mouth that would have an impact on your business.

In this sense, video sharing is also a handy tool. A video that shouldn't be an out-of-the-botox marketing ad, but a smart way to fix an issue would undoubtedly hit the jackpot with a sophisticated Facebook audience. It would sound more welcoming and thus draw rather than repel people at first glance.

Another essential tool that can be easily overlooked is the gathering of like-minded individuals who can help expand your company. This should not be confused with business groups or societies. You may also consider certain forms of participants of groups or communities. Members who do not exactly help to promote something actively, but only find something that would support them so that they would hold on to it; thus, it is essential to gather around people who have the same passion for pursuing a particular cause. You can provide the edge of the Facebook market themselves and extend your scope to a degree previously unmanageable.

Among the other essential yet easily overlooked strategies is the very nature of networking. Remember that Facebook is a social site; thus, of what is in the service or product that could be viewed in the form of something beneficial to that virtual community. This is where these group marketing clicks usually. If it is handled correctly, it could get on and spread like wildfire's.

Sticking to your ethics is what's going to get you a fair deal. Beware of venturing into anything that could lead your messages to be dumped in the spam folder. Tell yourself what it's like you'd instead drop there. It would have been more comfortable for you to understand it then.

Apart from this, we also need to keep a constant eye on what's new in the virtual market. To do this, it is essential that you keep track of the network and that your system is helping you out here. In this way, business ethics is the same as anywhere else. You've got to be a step ahead of the market, in this case, the virtual world.

Facebook has on its pages or profiles specific segments of the market. Almost all fields of business, be they financial or legal or consumer goods or travel or real estate or insurance, you name them, and they are on Facebook. This should, therefore, be no surprise that there are dedicated websites that direct people to different ways and methods of using this platform for the best of results. Looking at these pages would do no good to improve your chances, but it also depends on your understanding as a business professional.

Including targeting, there are also old ways of direct marketing, such as placing the banner on Facebook or one-liner. The prospect of reaching over two hundred million people in such a fashion could easily seem to appeal to anyone to do so, but here again, the concept should never be over. It could turn the fire on the brand if people start to get irritated.

Some firms deal with the processing of emails from Facebook users, and they can also be approached for a mutually beneficial connection. Getting email IDs from so many people from different parts of the world could prove to be a vital tool in your search for expansion, but here again, the key is the correct use. The approach is what predetermines the deal, and if you click with the recipient, then you can reap the rewards far more than you could imagine.

You can also set up a Facebook fan page. This fan page is a public profile that empowers the brand with its growing fan base. This allows users to connect and collaborate with Facebook users to expand their virtual market presence. But any such fan page should have a specific vision and content analysis, what you want to show, and to what degree you want to share with your prospective customers and clients. Constant page update is also essential, as is the face of your brand.

Different promotions may also be used to drive business and generate traffic to the fan page or company profile page. For example, you can run a strategy that offers' n' rewards to people who have successfully expanded the reach of the page between their friends and network connections by making them a member of the profile or a fan page. It helps to grow your fan base and, as a result, you could easily carry out any survey with better results that would suit your intent in the real sense. You could also use the study or its resources as incentives or as opportunities to produce more participants. You need to keep all sorts of people in mind, it might just be that fans of your page might need a little more than what they're getting to support your page, or others might be offering something, and they'd be drawn to that, so why would you risk such a thing for less. Therefore, because it is advisable to provide an incentive, it does not necessarily have to be monetary, but it has to be sufficiently attractive.

Caring for current registered customers is as critical as looking for new ways and means of creating new ones, if not more. If only one were to keep himself occupied with the former, his requirements would suffice, as these on roll customers would slowly but steadily and eventually expand the scope if they were satisfied. They'd do it sooner rather than later because there's nothing more contagious than a happy customer.

Finally, it should be understood that Facebook is at the same time, a device and a culture. The trick is to strike the right balance between the two and to reap the rewards for a long time.

Chapter 13: Instagram Marketing Tips for Your Business

Millions of people now use Instagram worldwide. Instagram has simplified taking pictures and sharing them with friends, and many people enjoy it. In addition to networking, Instagram can be used more effectively for marketing. Instagram is a great promotional tool that you can use online to promote your product.

Note that the story is worth a thousand words with photos and videos, Images, and Instagram is all about images. If you're on Instagram for marketing purposes, you should know that random pictures don't work. You must continuously post pictures of your items. Posting your product photos is one of the best ways to raise awareness of your brand and increase the sales of your products. The pictures don't need to be very accurate. The critical thing is that the images highlight the main characteristics and functions of the goods you endorse. The photos will attract a broad audience on Instagram.

Videos are also critical in the marketing of Instagram. To promote the product at hand, you should create and share a video with your employees. You can also choose to make a live video review of the product and share it with Instagram.

Photos and videos are more appealing than text files to many men. Online records are more likely to become viral when people share them. These are more unforgettable than text files as well. Build photos and videos to demonstrate the story and values of your company. Therefore, images and videos are critical if your brand and sales are to improve.

Use quality media

It would help if you had high-quality pictures and videos in your feeds to increase your visibility — demand professional assistance or guidance from a photographer where applicable. You can nevertheless take sharp images with a great camera. Try to get the best view of your pictures. For better results, edit your pictures. Mobile phones are now fitted with tools for photo editing. Instagram has a range of photo editing tools as well. Apply these tools to your marketing intent on Instagram.

Connect with our supporters

Contact your customers is essential, particularly for the growth of businesses with a small market share. You can start by showing your customers that their input concerns you. You can do this by answering your questions and comments. It increases the value and trust created by the customer and enhances the exposure of your goods and businesses. Your followers of Instagram can influence your company's success significantly and should never be underestimated.

Use Hashtags

They are using hashtags. It would help if you used them because users of Instagram interact with hashtags. Hashtags enable users to search your content and are necessary if your followers are to be increased. Tags such as media can generate a viral impact that benefits your company. You can also use trendy hashtags, particularly if the hashtags are connected to your product. This is important because Instagram users can search for posts using hashtags.

Use branded hashtag

You should include your company name in your hashtags. Using particular hashtags for a specific promotional campaign you are running. This not only promotes your campaign but also gives your customers a unique hashtag to connect and share with others.

Have a friendly attitude to everyone

It would help if you recognized that Instagram is a group of persons with various ideas, emotions, and experiences when carrying out Instagram marketing. Be always polite to everyone, and enjoy your time connecting to you on your profile. Make sure you listen to your customers.

Be active

Post at least once a day to ensure that everything is up to date and your followers are updated with current events. You can try posting at different times of the day to see when your posts do best.

Consistency

To Instagram marketing, continuity is vital. Be consistent in your posts and develop a prominent subject in your posts. Let your followers know what you can expect.

Link your Instagram and Facebook accounts

Link your Instagram and Facebook accounts to maximize marketing power, link your Instagram and Facebook accounts. Now, on your Facebook page, you can have an Instagram tab. You can thus share your Instagram posts with your Facebook followers if you have a fan page.

You can network via Instagram with friends and the planet. For marketing purposes, Instagram can be used. Instagram marketing will enhance the exposure of your brand, raise your awareness, and thus increasing your revenue. Find the marketing above tips for success on Instagram.

How to Use Instagram With Your Direct Sales Business

Optimizing the Instagram channel for direct sales would offer tremendous rewards.

This article will cover how Instagram can be used in your direct marketing business. The purpose of this article is to turn your Instagram account into a revenue opportunity.

By overlooking the fundamentals of Instagram marketing, you encourage competition to succeed.

Instagram marketing increases the traffic on your website and the number of views per month. Yes, Instagram is so healthy! (source: affiliatemarketing.com) These are the top tips below for all affiliate marketers. If you're trying to sell your direct sales items using Instagram, you need to keep reading.

#1: Tell People What to Do

Nothing will help your business grow faster than asking your customers what you want them to do. This is a call for action. It works, it's time tested, and it's real. In the fast-paced world of social media, you need to show your followers how you can support them. Then you tell them right away where to go to get that help. In reality, your audience would appreciate the "right to the stage" tactics.

From our first-hand experience, Instagram is a unique social media channel in this regard. A typical person on Instagram will look at the picture, review the explanation, and follow the call to action. Easy as that, man. To make sales on Instagram, you need to call the operation "Click the link in the profile if you want to know more!" from practice when the call to action precedes the fantastic offer, you get more leads.

Sounds impressive right, huh? Okay, guess what, huh? It's working.

There are a lot of ways to attract your audience. It all begins by putting the right photos and calling for action out there. This leads to the #2 tip.

#2. **Identify Your Audience's Preference**

Photos that appeal to the customer's expectations is the essential step in monetizing the Instagram business.

Identifying, engaging, and staying relevant to your audience is a crucial factor. And whether you make the most of the revenue from this network.

Identifying the needs of your audience is a big issue. I've seen what happens when business owners publish the base material to the audience they want. Let's agree that this isn't good!

Luckily, you're reading this with some knowledge of the tastes of your audience. So it's supposed to be easy. Take a look back at your Instagram feed and check out the popular posts. What did you receive comments, shares, and likes? Your target will have the same tastes and preferences as you do. Start every Instagram post with the question, "Would this picture interest me?" "Should I purchase this one?" If you answer yes, then you've found great material.

Consider going to the websites of your rival as well. Check out some of their popular posts and photos. When you find images that your target audience is engaging with, make them identical for your website.

Once you've set your audience's preferences, it's time to move to tip #3.

#3 Identify Benefit Locations

The monetization opportunities for Instagram remain limited while you serve a direct sales business. Most direct sales companies do not permit their affiliates to take out advertising space. Read the fine print on your membership. The chances are good that paid advertising is not approved.

So what the heck are you going to do?

Recall the tip #1? The call to action, huh? Your affiliate situation requires you to use a compelling call to take action at a benefit venue.

Just wait a minute. Don't post your affiliate connection to this venue, create an exciting freebie instead. Your goal is to bring the viewer to content. You can post this freebie link to Instagram and any social network. This connection is going to collect email leads from people who want more information.

What's the content? Content is the knowledge that your target audience wants. If you serve the make-up industry, then a freebie on how to contour is a good option. If you serve the health and wellness sector, low-fat recipes will work.

These benefit locations aim to take your audience to Instagram and turn them into leads. In the definition, call the action to "Click the link in the profile." This is the location of your profit. First, you switch from a benefit position to a selling enclosure. Please keep reading for tip #4.

#4: **Educate, Bring Variety, and Repeat**

After you've taken your audience to a benefit spot, you need an action plan. Take the lead you wanted your freebie and convert it into a product sale.

Here's an approach that uses three different features.

Start with your schooling.

A lead who wants your freebie is a "freebie-seeker'. They will never buy until you know about your valuable goods.

Offer them the knowledge they need and build confidence.

Give a variety of leads.

A key to bridging the lead to a sale is to introduce a multi-step follow-up sequence. Develop a marketing plan that includes email marketing, promotions, and helpful graphics. Think of infographics that teach the goods a new technique. Variety also means that you include invitations to webinars or other live events. This is the key to getting them to selling; what works for some people won't work for others. You need to be sufficiently diverse to collect revenue from various personalities.

Repetition.

Individuals have to hear the same message 12 times on average before it enters. You can feel exhausted from repeating the product information over and over. Comprehensible. But you must know that the first time your customers haven't noticed you. The second or third or fourth time, they haven't heard from you! Do not make the mistake of thinking that your "before and after" photo on Instagram would sell you. The aim of Instagram marketing leads to a sales environment. This is where you talk to them all the time. Had the viewer first heard the sales pitch, you would have had thousands of sales already. Since they don't, they probably won't hear your message. Delete them from the social media site by calling them to practice. Guide them to a' benefit platform.' Place a variable marketing campaign in place and speak to them again and again and again and again.

#5 Research & Optimization

Testing & optimization must be a major component of Instagram's strategy. You need to grasp two different analytical techniques. Qualitative and subjective (measurement) (non-measurement).

Quantitative

Here's where each image/post can be measured. Build (or use the analytical app) to measure each post's interaction.

The number of clicks to your link in the profile will be your desired measurement.

You want to measure how many clicks have been converted into a lead (they have given you an email). Quantitative analysis indicates the potential revenue. You have a good starting point if each lead supports your marketing campaign (tip #4).

Your objective is to make successful ads for Instagram. The more information you can apply to this report, the more productive you are.

Day/day post·

Content type link, photograph, video, etc.·

Link ratio for lead captures.

Use this technique to create an image of the productivity of actions and the waste of time.

Qualitative

The qualitative analysis looks at aspects that are not numbers of your marketing. Your qualitative research includes your company's aesthetics.

Here are a few questions to start with.

Am I supplying sufficient information?

Will my material help my efforts (to call people to action)?

Does my freebie link work well for Instagram?

Do I come across as a "spammer," despite everything I know about marketing? ·

Am I giving my target market true value?

One of the key criteria should be certain qualitative assessments. Are you paying sufficient attention to your service, or are you just trying to make a buck? Trust us. Believe us. People know the difference between a salesman and a valuable leader.

The only way to sell is to be the interested master in qualitative analysis first. The more value you give, the more success you have. This is a long process. It can be safe to advertise your direct sales goods actively in social media. Support us again. Take the time to be the value leader, and you will earn more in the long run.

You have read five tips to pay for your company's direct sales with Instagram.

1. Tell people what they should do

2. Identify the interests of your audience

3. Identify the place of benefit

4. Training, diversity, and repetition

5. Analysis and optimization

Chapter 14: Pinterest Marketing

Consider using Pinterest as part of your marketing strategy if you use social media to promote your company.

Questions to ask to help determine whether marketing with Pinterest can be of value to your business:

• Is your company B 2B or B2C? Evaluation of the Pinterest option

• Are you going to use Pinterest to increase traffic?

• Is your target client primarily male or female?

• How do you think Pinterest can support you?

• Is your company, product, or service-based?

• Are your goods or services mainly related to fashion, marriage, cuisine, or crafts? »

• Do you have a strong visual appeal for your products? (Do you have time to improve your website and other social media sites' content and visual quality, mainly photos?)

• Are you already using business social media?

• Why would you like to use Pinterest

- You want to pin things that don't entirely apply to your company (news, trends, ideas of others, etc.)?

If you have straightforward answers to all these questions, you can find value in creating a social media presence based on Pinterest. However, you may set Pinterest aside for a while when you are overwhelmed, annoyed, or burnt out on' another social media site.'

What do you know about Pinterest?

Pinterest has a slightly different social media feature. It's not the spot where you similarly refer to Facebook or Twitter, and it's not another blog. Pinterest is a social and visual "virtual pinboard" that allows users to post (pin) pictures or web videos on their boards and explore Pinterest.

Once a Pinterest account has been developed, a virtual board can be classified within that account, and the user can add explanations to show why an image or video has been saved. Many (but not all) pictures/pins link the user to the website source for easy later access. The account owner-user can invite others to pin or limit material of related interest only to personal use.

One journalist views Pinterest as a' directory of intentions.' A person often uses his Pinterest board to collect ideas about something, primarily visual images. You might want to see pictures of wedding vests, for example (a popular topic on Pinterest). The board may be "pinned" with images of interest.

Many photos from the website include a Pin It button on their pages that allows the user to access the contents of this website. And users can upload their content–the beautiful dessert, a newly completed oil painting picture, or pictures of the new winter fashion accessories.

How does marketing go about that?

As an entrepreneur, the goal is to increase the traffic of visitors to your social media site. Once there, the web content is responsible for motivating tourists to shop. Pinterest is now seen as an addition to website corporation, with an increase of 29 percent in the group.

Etsy's increasingly popular online marketplace is one of Pinterest's most performing brands, increasing Etsy's sales by 9.4% in 2013. Why the interest? Why the interest? These are the videos!

People love photos on do-it-yourself (DIY) projects in advertising and are posted using crafts, how-to, and recipes.

Viewers want images on every site. Brands must include images in Pinterest and all social media websites that are used for marketing.

- Knowledge—Start by building your knowledge base on Pinterest's interests and prospective customers.

- More than 70 million users on Pinterest. This is a broad customer/consumer opportunity base.

- Women users repin to their boards (pinning photos found on the Internet and in Pinterest search) more often than men but have fewer followers.

- DIY, art, hair, and beauty and fashion are the top three Pinterest categories.

- Babies, beauty, art, fashion, fitness, food, home decor, baby, pets, and travel are the most common categories in Pinterest. Seasonal topics are also prevalent—vacation, seasonal changes, current events.

- The type of use varies considerably from men to women: women concentrate on fewer categories, while men scatter their sticks. The top five women's groups also account for 56% of all their Pinterest activities; the senior five men's categories are under 40%.

- Men consumers prefer categories of photography, sculpture, architecture, and home decor.

- Pinning time can be crucial. The best time to pin is between 14:00 and 16:00 (East time), while the best time to pin is between 8:00 and 1:00 (Eastern time).

Conduct extensive research online. See some of the famous retail sites and see how they use PinIt widgets. Look for topics in one of the most common categories on the Internet. Your quest is likely to show ties to Pinterest. Click and display the text and study material, layout, and appearance on the website of Pinterest.

Build a Pinterest account and search through the business section of the website. You can customize your Pinterest boards privately and change them before you think you are ready to show them. Then« adjust the view status and begin to track the results of your PinIt.

You will have access to some useful resources, including analytics. Use the analytics tool to view information about pin activity on your website and Pinterest boards. Analytics will help you understand better through pinners ("Most repinned and most clicked"). For further conversions, customize and fine-tune your sticks.

Your customers will explore your website to pin items and replenish them with other Pinterest boards. You will focus on creating content that represents the interests of your customers. Typically, Pinterest users share content that has educational value and practicality. How can you match your content with the needs of customers?

• Website review: Is your website pictures accessible, up-to-date, and up-to-date content rich in quality pictures, in particular? Get a good order for your website.

• Content Management—Organize all your Pinterest boards according to themes to make finding and viewing specific content easier for other users.

• Brand images—Researchers have noted that pinner switches are large watermarks over pictures.

• Shopper-friendly content-Pinterest is about shopping more than most social media sites.

That board should shopper-friendly content: Pinterest is buying more than most social media sites. Each board should be "shopper-friendly" built and full of content. Describe the product or service and only use clear images of quality.

• Join the community—you spend time reading, tracking, and communicating with the people in the groups every day: asking and answering questions, commenting on the material of others.

• Repin-When it comes to Pinterest directly, invite others to repin your board material. Repinning to your account reminds you of the person you answered from (the person receiving a note or an e-mail). The person from whom you answered can also offer the repin favor.

• No broken backlinks—make sure your Pinterest links backlink correctly to your blogs, Facebook, or Twitter. Repair some backlinks are broken!

Image Clear Pictures Let's get clear. Several vital points around sharing Pinterest pictures and videos are more likely to be known: • Product photographs (on Pinterest) will be repeated if the image does not include a face—23% more likely. BTW, one study showed that Pinterest's faceless pictures are 4.25 times higher.

• Multi-color pictures are favored. Objects in red, orange, and brown are twice as replicated; objects in blue are less likely. Medium-light photographs are repeated twenty times as often as black images, eight times as much as white ones.

• Background and texture-influence choices for repinning. Pinster prefers images with a background of less than 30 percent; the "down" rate for photos with a background value of 40% or more was two to four times. Smooth textures are favored over rough surfaces—with up to 17 repins.

• Picture scale—studies show that larger images and vertical images are responsible. Further small photos and infographics are selected because of the difficulty of reading from the

Pinterest page. The infographic headline is essential for more clicks.

- Traffic response-you can monitor traffic response by including a special call for action on the pin landing page. Keep your presence. A large company with its marketing group or consultants can spend a considerable amount of time researching ROI analyses, putting professional and text photographs, and updating content almost daily.

The smaller company member will spend at least two hours per day, track reviews, reply to comments (when necessary), and update content. It is a relatively short time and effort commitment to producing potentially good outcomes.

Over time, the comments and number of visitors will start showing which areas of your content are valid, such as the products that are ignored and bought. In comparison, they can show a lack of interest and a limited number of purchases.

If your traffic remains sluggish, evaluate all aspects—text, layout, pictures, and links—all. You may want to or need to consult an online marketer or web/media designer to help update your content.

It is quick to overwhelm audiences with knowledge and over-saturation that is as important in marketing. Feedback will once again let you know what works and what doesn't work.

Once again, advertisers will buy "likes" and "tweets" to inflate the numbers of actual audience likes and tweets. You might not want the high numbers to be an accurate representation of who follows a brand. Most significantly, the sales relevant to that brand are not reliable.

Pinterest Marketing Tricks

Pinterest is one of the best platforms to attract large amounts of traffic to your website. It also allows you to connect 176,000,000 users free of charge. Yes, surveys have shown that 18% of Pinterest users have $75,000 or more in total. It means that you can target potential customers for your company.

Also, with Pinterest power, you can use pictures, private messages, and videos to bring people to your website, YouTube videos, or any posts you choose. You can, therefore, bring massive traffic to your landing page where you can build up massive subscribers daily for your company.

Remember, it will always be your recipe. Visitors—-> Build Subscribers— > Prospective Consumers—-> Building Relationships—> The Business Revenue. This is precisely Pinterest Marketing's strength.

Here are a few tricks and strategies for the right path:

Tricks#1: Blast Emails in your file. Instead of following others on Pinterest, send emails to your list and let them know that on your Pinterest page, you can share cool tips and tricks on how to solve their problems.

Trick #2: Follow 300 Pinterest users every day on your niche. Although this strategy is a little old, it will, in reality, encourage other people to join you on Pinterest.

Trick #3: pin 30 to 40 photos daily. But, in your niche, you have to rely on those consumers. Although this is a wide-ranging technique, it will help you to access your Pinterest page.

Trick #4: Delete users who don't follow you back from Pinterest. You have to wait about a week before you uninstall any Pinterest users you follow. Why does this matter? Okay, you only want to deal with users who are going to communicate with you.

Trick #5: On your website, put a Pinterest button. It enables other Pinterest users to share your blog or squeeze post freely.

Trick #6: Add Pinterest pictures as your journey. You should add to your Pinterest a regular image to tell your followers what you do every day. This allows your audience to see photographs of your daily activities.

Trick #7: Greet every new Pinterest follower. This gives you a lasting impression of every audience that could be potential clients for your enterprise.

Trick #8: Make friends with some users on Pinterest. Why does that matter? Okay, you will work together to pin each other posts when you make friends with ten leading Pinterest marketers. It enables you to create viral traffic between businesses.

You can add your name every time you post on Instagram.

Trick #9: Take pictures of some of Pinterest's friends. The principle is similar to Trick #8. The idea is to make sure you appeared famous to your audience. HINT: You can always take photos with the participants.

Trick #10: Apply the signature file to each email that comes out. You have something like. "P.S. You can track my every move in{{ Your PINTEREST URL}} on Pinterest."

Trick #11: Create a special offer on behalf of Pinterest to join you. Create* SPARK* and incentives to follow you on Pinterest for your audience.

Example: Create an event to ask the public to click on "Subscribe" to get a 90% discount coupon code at $99 for your most recent purchase. (Now, whether it's a $99 product or a $10 product doesn't matter. My point ..."Use the special discount."

Trick #12: Every Pinterest post in your niche is commented on. — Only the topics in your niche can you comment on. For example: If you're in the niche of weight loss, comment on the post in that niche. Whether you remain focused on this particular niche, you will optimize the results.

Trick #13: Having a cash market. You can use* real* cash as part of your contest, where you ask people to follow you or talk to them about Pinterest. You can also provide a* gift certificate* that you can use to buy your product.

Example:

- 1st Winner= $100 + $500 YOURPRODUCTS Gift Certificates.
- 2nd Winner= $75 + $400 YOURPRODUCTS Gift Certificates.
- 3rd winner= $50 + $250 YOURPRODUCTS Gift Certificates.
- 4th Winner= $25 + $150 YOURPRODUCTS Gift Certificates.
- 5th Winner= $75 YOURPRODUCTS Gift Certificates.

Trick #14: First, mark your name. Branding your name like JohnDoe is significant. I allow you to build your image as a public figure in which you draw loyal supporters.

For instance: < a goal= "blanco" rel="nofollow "href="http:/Pinterest.com / johndoe" > http:/Pinterest.com / johndoe</a > is much better than < a goal="blanco" rel="nofollow "href="http:/Instagram.com / xyscorp"> http:/Instagram.com / xyzcorp >

Trick #15: mark your company with your brand name. The following is an excellent example of this. — First, let people know. Once you do, people will want to learn about your company and your company's progress.

Recall: The dream of Pinterest is all about posting photos and videos. It means you are making a higher commission when you mark YOU with pictures and videos. It helped people to connect to your business. It's this important!

Trick #16: Schedule your weekly posts before time. — Rather than scheduling your weekly posts every day. You must send all posts for a single week at a time. In this way, you can stay unbeaten in other tasks for your company.

Trick #17: Buyer keywords target at all costs. At all costs. — Which one is rentier? Wedding advisors or research at the wedding?

1. When someone chooses the wedding consultant, do you think that a person is ready to buy?

2. If someone selects "wedding pieces," do you find that person available to purchase?

The answer is obvious, of course. If people select a "family counselor," they look for a specialist. That means they're READY for. My point is to take a closer look at your niche. It helps you to concentrate instead of just a pot of cauldron on a pot of gold.

Trick #18: At all costs, track your link. You lose cash if you don't follow. It's easy to feel you have no time. Nevertheless, if you cannot monitor your connection, you cannot know which clicks generate more and which wall post gives you a lower conversion.

Trick #19: Always use your Profile Summary Squeeze Site URL. — It allows you to build your Pinterest subscriber base. Keep in mind that your Pinterest marketing target is first to create your list. NOTE: Studies have shown that every user you have is $1 to $1.50 for your company monthly.

Trick #20: Always use photos that reflect on your audience's performance. Images are better than words. Use it to show the audience what it can do if it uses your products and services.

Trick #21: You can always publish the picture with a motivational quote if you have nothing new to share. Motivating quotes with so many negativities around us will draw the fans to follow you on Pinterest. (Yes, as often as you can, you can always use gram motivational quotes!)

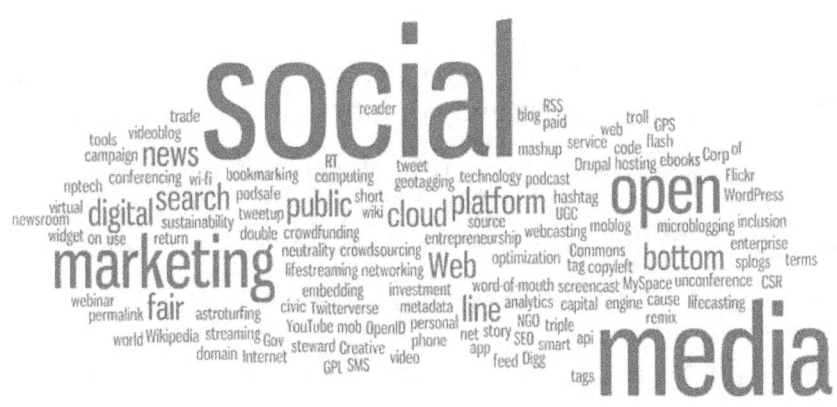

Chapter 15: Twitter Marketing

The marketing landscape is now shaped by different Internet channels that are available to attract customers worldwide.

Some of these online devices were not designed for marketing but recently found a niche in this field.

Entrepreneurs have possibilities that they never dreamt of having at their disposal.

One of the tools not for marketing, but a social network, is Twitter.

Twitter is a large community of interacting with people who are already educated about the internet.

This is the perfect combination to promote your company, your brand, or anything you have to give.

Start by creating a Twitter account, and you will conquer the Twitter world!

First, you should develop a marketing plan that includes your company's strategies and goals.

You should include information on how the business will be portrayed and the deals you have.

Right strategies should be used that present the business with a subtle approach in a positive light.

If you are too violent, you create negative consequences, and you don't want or expect to.

Provide credible explanations for why the consumer will purchase your product and, if possible, include any feedback.

A healthy marketing plan will help you get on the right track and reap the benefits of higher sales and profits.

Creating an overview of your business status is critical when designing marketing strategies that allow you to achieve your goals.

Twitter offers a range of useful tools to help you track the traffic to your website, your fans, their tweets, and further information to help you manage your publicity campaign better.

You can learn immediately how your business is rated, what your company followers think, and how satisfied your customers are.

You can change and adapt your strategies with this wealth of information.

Another significant advantage of Twitter is that you can reach your customers directly.

This is important for business because it provides more personal contact with these customers.

Customers who are happy and satisfied spread the word and provide you with man's most effective word-of-mouth ads.

Customers want to purchase online on account of their tight schedules and stressful deadlines so that if they can get to your Twitter company, they can have your business in their pocket.

Your traffic will multiply through springs and limits and revenues. This is an ongoing project that you will develop and execute carefully. When you have a plan with strategies and goals, you want to start to consider the audience you want and how you will achieve that. Right tactics should carry out the solid plan you have in place and enforce it.

You will take your photo more quickly on your Twitter account.

It will make the business feel personal, and your consumers will not feel as if they are talking to a corporation or unknown individual.

Always create your Twitter organic carefully; consumers can read it to see who you are and what your company is. Maintain it simple, short, and articulate.

Your Twitter account will work more smoothly for you with a few other marketing tools.

You are using Hootsuite.com and Tweetdeck.com to change schedules and to post social media messages simultaneously through social media platforms such as Facebook, Twitter, and Linkedin.

Hootsuite helps you to plan tweets without charge in advance. Some days it might be hard for you to be on Twitter, so this app helps you to schedule a tweet every time you want to share an idea or find a link you want to address.

Such tools will also allow you to manage your Twitter account and activities more efficiently and can help you submit messages while you work on another part of your business.

You need to be as educated and up to date as possible to succeed in business on the internet.

You have to keep up with the latest news, fads, and developments that sometimes happen very quickly.

Your fundamental marketing strategy with Twitter must be customer interaction.

A Twitter user wants to provide his input and views as part of your advertising campaign. Twitter facilitates this contact, and this engagement can help to gain the trust of your customers.

This is one of Twitter's most powerful principles.

You can use Twitter as a useful marketing tool for your business by following a few simple steps.

Follow people like you who are already interested in your company.

Millions of Twitter users are added every day, and many of them have a problem to solve for their product.

Connecting with those people who are interested in what you have to say is extremely important. Most customers tend to follow a person they asked to follow from; you can retrieve in this consumer audience that is looking for your product.

Remember that Twitter is a networking website; the basis for involvement is an exciting conversation.

You don't want to be desperate; get consumers to talk about what you have to sell.

Please don't be so cynical that with a sales pitch, you are pushing them away.

When you're trying to market your product to someone you don't know well, you must be courteous, respectful and cautious. Establishing a dialog at the outset will work much better than approaching followers with a high-pressure pitch that loses them immediately.

Online business is very similar to traditional business: nobody likes a salesman at high pressure! Take your time and cultivate loyal customers who tell their friends about your company and spread the right positive message.

Perhaps you can not use the proverbial handshake, but the product will be just as deserving of a kind, strong statement.

Tweet your followers often. Out of reach is a ubiquitous adage of Facebook.

Tweets have a short life, and consumers don't see you if you don't tweet.

Your customers know that your company is alive and well and that you still deliver the same quality products and services if you tweet regularly. At least once a day tweeting, research shows that under 10% of followers on Twitter go back to what was tweeted yesterday

If you're not consistently around, you're going to lose your focus. Be a regular Twitter presence.

Viral marketing campaign edition from Twitter is retweeting!

You will bring tremendous value and encourage ongoing talks as retweets propagate across Twitter. You will also draw thousands of new customers with retweets; the viral marketing plan will go on and go on.

This wave of information and information will be a dynamic force for your product to generate businesses and profits. One of the best ways to get more retweets is to post tweets on "how-to" topics.

Everybody loves learning how to do projects, and you can build a broad retweeting campaign by sharing this kind of information.

In this failing world, people try to do their projects, and you can provide the information that their work must be done on a cost-effective and timely basis.

Enter links to your website that can give you additional information on the subject and any related product you sell.

This will increase your profits because you share your expertise.

Research shows that conducting polls on Twitter can attract traffic and the business to your Twitter page with excellent incentives for participants. Everybody likes something free and can draw multiple supporters and fans, increasing their potential customer base.

This is a simple idea that can help you build a chart for your marketing strategies in other campaigns.

Another tactic is to connect all your social networking accounts with Twitter.

Your marketing campaign is better and more productive with the user base following all of these social sites.

You will leave no stone unturned in cyberspace.

With the amount of daily usage coupled with the constant connection with smartphones to social media sites, the advertising dollars receive rewards that you had never dreamed of.

Your company will be open 24/7 in countries around the world, and your successful business will never start with the sun.

Do not reinvent the wheel. Do not reinvent the wheel.

You will expand your Twitter awareness by reading other success stories and investigating Twitter marketing opportunities.

Learn different tips that benefited them when they started and what worked for them.

If this doesn't work for them, mark it off and continue to the next approach.

Using the best practices of those before you simplifies your journey and saves you precious time and money.

Link your Twitter campaign to traditional marketing.

You will have to remind each company that you now have a Twitter account.

Here you can find useful details and any deals that you give to your customers.

On all your business cards and other traditional marketing devices, place your Twitter link.

This is an effective way to keep customers up-to-date on trends, products, and other useful information.

The consumer will see your company as a success if you use the technologies you know about to support your business.

Once you get to know Facebook, take part in Twitter talks.

These are regularly scheduled meetings and are coordinated by a moderator. That chat has a subject of interest to the participants.

Sometimes a visiting guest tends to answer questions and respond to followers at a professional level. At the end of the session, a valuable transcript of the chat will be given. Twitter chats can provide you a great way to establish new relationships with people of similar interests to you.

You will identify potential customers and communicate with them as an authority on the subject; this will build confidence and trust in you and the product you deliver.

More people will notice you and expand your follower list that can generate more business. This indeed confirms your expertise in this area

Followers who engage in these daily chats are already heavily involved in the niche. They can provide you with a wealth of information and additional links, tips, and resources for your company.

This allows your potential customer to see a cyber face behind a product that increases leads and contacts.

One of the most significant opportunities on Twitter is to go back.

You want users to follow you, but many users you follow can gather from. If you don't follow anyone, you can send a message that you are only for sales and promotions on Twitter.

This is a selfish message that will not produce positive results; you will not generate a collective allegiance.

The following is a possible indication of care and consideration, which in the marketing plan should not be ignored.

Use Twitter's @mentioned feature to help you develop stronger ties and attract a more oriented audience.

This tool directs the tweet to a particular user and works more like a one-on-one approach.

Your goal is not to quickly sell a product; it is an appeal to action that requires them without the burden of a sales pitch.

You build a relationship that can produce a sale after the relationship has been created.

Such relationships will grow with time and patience and will react, retweet, and communicate with you more often.

Genuine business opportunities come from real relationships, which is a powerful tool to consider as you start your Twitter Marketing campaign. You can introduce these people to your advertising or company site as you contact the audience on Twitter. By building more confidence and trust in you, your users will begin to explore who you are on the market and what your product can do for you.

Post advertising with shortened URLs to guide you to your website.

If your information is relevant and exciting, you can explore your product further.

Tweet swaps are another feature of Twitter that you can use as a tool in your marketing toolbox.

It looks like ad swaps when you are advertising on the list of another person and advertising on your list. Your Twitter fans are listed to know more about you, read your messages, and educate them on current trends in their favorite niche.

You will not sell with tweet swaps; you will only develop ideas and drive traffic.

This will increase your visibility and allow you to grow a loyal, long-term follow-up that makes money for your business. You can access followers of others using tweet swaps and capture them with your ideas and deals.

Consider a Twitter buddy with a niche close to yours.

It would help if you were similar to your marketing strategies, but not the same.

Don't just look for someone with a massive list of followers; you want consistency in quantity, or the followers won't do you any good. The best idea is to offer these followers a free product instead of trying to sell them a product immediately. This method is for lead generation and not a sales promotion.

One of the fascinating ways to learn more about Twitter is to post questions on any topic, but preferably one about which you have a wealth of knowledge.

In your conversations with your fans, you will answer these questions. It establishes you as an authority on the subject and helps to build trust and reliability between you and your fans.

Starting a friendly but challenging dialog with others will build a community of followers that listen to your tweets and respond with their helpful ideas and thoughts.

It is a subtle way to promote your product by using the carefully collected information. Knowledge is power, and you want to have the power of Twitter marketing.

While your marketing plan is not correct or wrong, you will abide by the unwritten rules that guarantee successful promotion and great reviews when engaging with your followers

The right Twitter label will help to build loyal relationships that increase your sales and profit

Develop a plan with the amount of time you spend on your Twitter account.

Often it is easy to waste time and end a conversation you started with your followers in the wee hours of the morning.

Grant your followers plenty of time to post their material on Twitter.

Keep as close as possible to your schedule and make the most of any interaction you participate in.

The 80-20 concept of marketing applies both to Twitter marketing and traditional methods of promotion. Nobody wants to talk to you about topics if you continuously talk about yourself or promote your product.

You can include tweets on topics closely connected with your company, provide useful information to improve others ' lives and hold fascinating discussions on a variety of issues.

Offer various tweets when engaging with your supporters; don't promote yourself or your company.

A business relationship is like in other relationships, a two-way street.

It would help if you showed an interest in your customers to gain trust and trust before they buy a product from you.

Cross supports the marketing campaigns you use on your Twitter account. Use and integrate all tools available on the web so that they work for you smoothly and efficiently.

Link your email and URLs with any tweet you make so a follower can reach you more easily outside the Twitter community.

Be very careful about the content of your tweets.

You want the public to see all that you tweet when you use your Twitter account to be a marketing strategy.

You have no idea where these tweets are circulated so that derogatory conversations are avoided.

Don't mention anything you wouldn't say in public on your Twitter account

Make sure you are too personal or familiar with your customers so that there is no mixed message.

Always be professional, honorable, and respectful of your language. Jokes and innuendos off-color are not appropriate.

Put other people's interests before your own.

You are not all about your Twitter marketing account; it is an opportunity to establish a quality relationship that will bring your company business and profits in the future. Take time to listen, appreciate, and share content, rather than force your views and ideas on others. Be interested and be polite.

One of the harshest aspects of your tweets is to use business terms or words that people may not understand or know.

With your audience interaction, you don't want to look disrespectful.

Do not use industry-specific rhetoric; it confuses the audience.

You have a brief time to understand your curiosity and attention; do not use terms that you need to look up or ask for them to describe.

You would not like to be a corporate robot whose goal is to sell a product and move on to the next customer.

Try to communicate with your potential customers effectively and confidently.

Don't condescend or sponsor them; they won't be enthusiastic about you and will switch to a more user-friendly person to communicate with.

Twitter is one of the most popular marketing tools today.

Seven Free Twitter Marketing Strategies

Although most people love and use Facebook as their preference for social media, Twitter has become a favorite among many professionals. The number of followers in social media, marketing campaigns, companies, media professionals, and celebrities has almost gained popularity. Ashton Kutcher and Britney Spears have more Twitter followers than the entire Swedish, Israeli, German, Ireland, Norwegian, and Panamanian populations. As I am very interested in social media, I always ask people what they think about Twitter. If they use it as a significant networking medium to support you, your brand, your produce, etc., some people don't know much about this increasingly popular tool and how to gain more visibility and use it without taking too long. In my specific fields, I use social media platforms to communicate with other professionals and business people, and you will note that some people choose to use Snapchat, not Facebook! The easiest way to spread across all channels is to find you faster. When you continue to use sites like Twitter and Facebook to easily reach the people who are looking for your products and services, you will hopefully start to attract a higher number of readers, a broader audience, and a profitable result in your home-based business.

The Huffington Post published an article recently sharing some interesting information about the number of Twitter users, what people are looking for, profiles of the site users, and how people sort, search and follow valuable content. According to the report, Twitter now reports that 8% of Americans use Twitter and have over 190 million people tweeting 65 million times a day. This is a HUGE audience to tap into for the domestic business manager or any other specialists! Hubspot has assembled a post in several sources using various graphs to illustrate 100 plus Twitter statistics.

As you can probably see-given these numbers, it's not that difficult to put yourself as a leader on Twitter. So long, so you concentrate on building your brand and adding value to others, there is no explanation why the number of followers you have gradually increased. You can sign up with TwitterCounter.com to test your info, and with the following seven strategies each day for the past three months, I have received about 10-15 new followers with the most 35 in a single day.

I ask random people a lot about Twitter, and the responses are fascinating. I think many people don't know how to use it and typically forget their profiles. Maybe they think it might take too long to keep up with their tweets. Often people react by saying to me, "Paul, I don't want a bunch of mad unknown people to follow me." Like a new follower who left them open to all their nasty secrets. My reaction is,' Don't just follow them back! Anyway, don't just concentrate on attracting supporters; this isn't necessarily the point of your marketing. You might end up with a bunch of "spam" supporters and not become closer to building relationships in your field with influential leaders and innovators worldwide through Twitter. Mostly, you want followers of consistency. How do you get them? How do you get them? Coherence, meaning, personality, and the seven free resources that follow. Now let's get into them.

Social Oomph Social Oomph's Seven Strategies #1 is an excellent little tool that has both a free application version and a $29.97/month "professional" version and a free 7-day trial. I've only used and considered the free version of the software indispensable. Some of the advantages include scheduling, archiving, and saving tweets to be used later if you wish to recycle the specific tweet.

Vet' the new folders that allow your account to check whether or not your new follower is a' spammer.' Creates and automates a message of direct welcome to your new folders.

To connect your tweets, you can add your other social accounts like Ping. Fm, your Blog, and Twitter.

The Seven Strategies

1. SocialOomph mainly to schedule my tweets so that they are posted without me having to be home. Take 10 minutes in the

morning to schedule 3 updates and syndicate all day long! Do three more as you sleep so that you can keep Europe and Asia up-to-date.

2. Twellow Another free registration service. Twellow is just what it sounds like—a Facebook yellow pages. It is a directory of hundreds of different categories of public twitter accounts and searches functions to help you find people in your niche. The platform has more than 30 million profiles registered. Some advantages include: Set up a full bio and user profile for viewing.

Join other users straight from the web quickly.

Add links to your other profiles on social media.

In the beginning, you can join ten categories to target your particular niche. I belong to several categories: network marketing, small businesses, entrepreneurs, yoga, spirituals, alternative medicine, theatre, social media, etc. I am now in 21 groups and subcategories.

An overall great place for those who share your interests to find and find!

3. Twitter-Karma This site will list all of your followers and your followers in the entire list. It's just a list of profile names and faces that helps you to' unfollow' someone who doesn't follow you. It will also demonstrate how they tweeted recently

and give you a sense of who is mindful of following people back. It's always lovely to return the favor, and if not,' Twitter Karma will get you. It will look right in front of you. Better get together, sweetheart. Join Facebook! Enter the Twitter race!

4. Hashtags. Org: This site allows you into your niche or subject matter to identify keywords and will provide you with information on tags, users, and trends. You are using hashtags to categorize your tweets to find your tweets in that niche. Make sense? Make sense? When, for example, you tweet about Network Marketing, you can add a hashtag (#) to the keyword's beginning. This will categorize your tweet into this category, so you can find tweets for #Network marketing yours when someone comes to Twitter. The idea is to make sure your niche will find you — not the opposite way.

5. Image Classifications: The customized context of your Twitter is an essential element for creating your brand across all platforms. You want to keep your image consistent, and Twitter lets you customize your copy. None of your photos contain links to other websites, but there is a lot of unused screen space for you to personalize your Twitter history more quickly. You can add additional photos, your website, social media icons, or more information about what you are doing.

For access generic free twitter backgrounds, you can try TwitterBackground.com. The other choice is to create your own or have somebody help you with design. If you are looking for an accomplished, talented graphic designer to help with your brand or logo, then look out for some stellar work by Scott Hartwig! See this article for more information on image dimensions.

6. Tweetdeck: You can see Twitter updates in real-time through this app. It is essentially a view of five columns that organizes your Twitter layout. These columns allow you to view recent tweets by all your contacts, recent tweets or nice mentions, direct messages, Twitter topics, and suggestions for TweetDeck. You can update all in one go to 6 different social media sites. Recently TweetDeck upgraded its system to ensure that users are no longer limited to 140 Tweets. The new TweetDeck design uses Deck. Ly to allow longer tweets. You can download it for free on Google Chrome, your desktop, or Android phones.

It will soon be on the iPad and the iPhone. With the new interface, you can now connect all your connections via Twitter, Facebook, Google Buzz, and Foursquare.

7. TwiTip Blog: Many blogs can be used to find truly informative social media strategies, tips, and news. Darren Rowse, the co-author of Pro Blogger and publisher of ProBlogger.net, founded TwiTip.com around 2005. TwiTip is a place for advice, news, and tools to improve Twitter use. Whether it is for personal reasons, to expand or extend your brand.

Final Exercise

Compile all the exercises you have completed in the handbook and incorporate the analysis in your business plan.

Conclusion

Thank you for making it through to the end of "*Make Money With Digital Marketing*", let's hope it was informative and able to provide you with all of the tools you need to achieve your goals whatever they may be.

The next step is to polish your business plan blocking all loopholes. Talk to a few professionals like business analysts and accountants to help fail-proof your plan and budget, respectively. When all is ready, pick a launch date. Yes, even online businesses launch officially before the online eyes of their prospects. This launch duration is to give you time and opportunity to build into your launch. Call it a pre-launch game where you create anticipation and grow an audience before your business takes off.

Prepare content materials for your pre-launch. Have a laid-out strategy that will ease into the launch date. Get blog posts ready, run popular topic discussions on your social media, create attractive graphics and post them, ask friends and family to check out your platforms and share your content, and give information about your company and what you will be offering.

Post upcoming products (use real and quality images) and give more information about them. Entice your prospects to yearn for purchase. Offer launch discounts and offers, or even chances to pre-order. When pre-launching, focus on quality, legitimacy, and giving valuable information. The pre-launch duration can be the ticket to faster success. Be smart!

Oliver J. Rich

www.ingramcontent.com/pod-product-compliance
Lightning Source LLC
Chambersburg PA
CBHW071351210526
45465CB00001B/57